Search for the True Aphrodisiac

Aphrodisiac

By Timothy Leary

RONIN PUBLISHING
BERKELEY CA

Ronin Books
by Timothy Leary

High Priest

Chaos & Cyber Culture

The Politics of Ecstasy

Psychedelic Prayers

Change Your Brain

The Politics of Self-Determination

Start Your Own Religion

Your Brain Is God

Turn On Tune In Drop Out

Musings on Human Metamorphoses

Evolutionary Agents

The Politics of PsychoPharmacology

Alternative to Involuntary Death

Search for the True Aphrodisiac

By Timothy Leary

Search for the True Aphrodisiac

PUBLISHED BY
Ronin Publishing, Inc.
PO BOX 22900
OAKLAND, CA 94609
www.roninpub.com

Production:

Editor: Beverly A. Potter

Cover Design: Brian Groppe

Book Design: Beverly A. Potter

Fonts: Allise—Fonthead, Avenir—Linotype, Dalliance—Emi-
gre, Jade—Swifle International, Navel—Fonthead, Venis—
Chank.

Some illustrations are by Pete Von Sholly from *The Game
of Life* by Timothy Leary.

Library of Congress Card Number: 2009933882
Distributed to the book trade by PGW/Perseus
Printed in the United States

Material in this book came from *Chaos & CyberCulture* and
The Game of Life by Timothy Leary, and from material created by Beverly Potter.

Table of Contents

Introduction

by V. Vale

A **society that does not recognize** and honor its prophets and truth-sayers is doomed. Timothy Leary was a prophet who years ago envisioned the way our "consensus reality" was morphing into our present-day computer/Internet-dominated world—where "virtual reality" seems to be taking precedence over so-called "real life." Collectively, our experiences are becoming more and more second-hand—electronic. Consequently, everything that constitutes the sphere of our sexual consciousness and activities cannot fail to be affected—at least, potentially. Anyone having access to a computer and the Internet can easily locate "free" graphic imagery and texts illuminating an extreme range of behavior and practices, from the most "vanilla" to the most kinky.

Since the Internet has lowered the financial bar giving practically "zero sum" access to texts and graphics depicting the most imaginative sexual fantasies and practices since the world began, what does this do to the human imagination? What can an individual think of that hasn't already been done by some-

In the relentless human quest for more and more liberation, liberty, and freedom, what are the new frontiers and boundaries to be explored and possibly extended?

one, somewhere? In the relentless human quest for more and more liberation, liberty, and freedom, what are the new frontiers and boundaries to be explored and possibly extended? Are there unlimited parameters to the human imagination in the sphere of sexual consciousness?

Early on, Tim Leary foresaw that the computer was a hardware/software extension of the human brain, mimicking the way the brain processes and stores knowledge. Just as psychedelic/mind-expanding drugs seemingly extended the range of the human imagination, so the computer might extend the range of imagery and also, through the global interconnectedness of the Internet, erase physical— or at least symbolic verbal/imagistic—boundaries between humans wishing to communicate and connect with others and thus expand the scope of their lives.

Hence the predictable rise of almost-unlimited erotic/ sexual images and words, updated and augmented on a daily basis, even on home computers. As almost everyone now can find everybody else interested in a specific fetish or special interest, a kind of hive mind has sprung up whereby ideas exponentially expand and develop. Humans developing sex machines can now find an international audience, and software code writers can craft 0s and 1s into userfriendly robotic interfaces that can be implemented globally by people speaking in different native tongues. Hence the now almost *passe* technology known as "teledildonics," whereby hardware "physically corresponding" to a woman's genitals can be manipulated by a partner who may be 23,000 miles away. Visual/verbal communication updating is maintained by webcams and microphones attached to their respective home computers outfitted with keyboards, trackballs, drawing tablets and other controllers.

The rise of pay-to-view voyeurcams has proliferated along with websites promising millions of images and thousands of videos. Millions?! You could die before you saw them all... And if you processed this data for half of your waking hours, did you then really "have a life" of your own—with your own unique imagery, fantasies, narratives and scripts? Where is your own unique identity in all this hurricane of mediated electronic images?

What is most overlooked with Tim Leary's seeming advocacy of recreational drug experimentation are his warnings as to the importance of "set" and "setting" to ensure a safe, glorious, wonder-filled "trip." And his repeated insistence that the brain is the primary erogenous zone. What constitutes true eroticism? Isabel Allende claimed, "For women, the best aphrodisiacs are words. The G-spot is in the ears. He who looks for it below there is wasting his time." Unique original poetic language, invented on the spot to inspire wondrous visions of hope, has won more hearts than all the sex technology invented to date.

Until the individual dream can be captured and saved to computer memory storage, the human imagination, with or without drugs and computers, will remain the ultimate, miraculous, cinerama-conjuring wonder machine capable of inspiring our most favorite memories and pleasurable recollections. And for each person alive on planet earth, memory is the supreme judge of a life lived. Who did you love? What were your favorite experiences to cherish and recollect in tranquility? What did you create that you are lastingly proud of? Those are the gold standards ... All else is dross.

Leary envisioned computers—like drugs—catalyzing a massive deployment of imagination-drenched creativity and pleasurable activities.

Tim Leary tried to give us gold. In a universal way, Leary envisioned computers—like drugs—catalyzing a massive deployment of imagination-drenched creativity and pleasurable activities. What better fate could be imagined? In this book, enjoy his speculations and appreciate the clairvoyance of his uniquely open mind, channeling a future bursting with increased pleasure, creativity, and liberty for all. If indeed the imagination creates the future, the more of us who imagine this, the likelier it may come to pass. Reading this book may help...

—V. Vale, Publisher
RE/Search Publications
researchpubs.com

Vale and his remarkable publishing house (have) produced an amazing series of books over the years and kept the flag of independent publishing flying during a very difficult time—the most consistently interesting publisher in America, without a doubt.

—J. G. Ballard

1

Ĭ Want You

Y **ou get away from me** with this locker-room jock talk," I replied. The selection of ovum and sperm is not an athletic contest, you fool. However wounding this may be to the male-scientist-ego, this most important step in the evolution of species is not a blind muscle-feat.

I surged out of my father's penis. I recall the pell-mell stampede of the macho-jacks pushing each other aside to rush up the fallopian tube. But I didn't join the race. My sperm-navigation manual told me that this was an aesthetic-intelligence test. So I was in no hurry. I floated along and discovered to my delight that Mom's recreational system was the most wondrous exciting environment! Cushy, velvet, pulsing with cellular information, surging with perfumed signals and chemical instructions. Tissue-temples and ovarian-architecture. And the incredible presence of a humming super-intelligence located at the end of the fallopian highway.

"While the jocks flailed away. I floated

I surged out of my father's penis.

along on the eggs and tidal waves—alertly sensitive to the knowledge I was picking up. "It seemed like eternities of blissful rapture. Finally the tide-tow floated more closer and closer to the goal. *The Egg!*

First, let me tell you of Her magnificence. The Ovum is fifty thousand times bigger than the sperm body. It can only be described as a sun—radiating light and powerful vibrations. As I approached I saw, to my surprise, that the Ovum, far from being a passive blob waiting to be penetrated   by the phallic sperm, was surrounded by magnetic fields and bristled with radar scanners and laser defenses. As each sperm plowed into this field it was scoped, studied, and then lasered into shriveled debris.

"This discovery confirmed my intuition not to rush in with macho zeal. I laid back, observing carefully the many sensory apertures, trying to decipher the electro-chemical signals that She was emitting. Trying to figure out what She liked, what She wanted.

After a while I sensed-felt a soft magnetic pull and proceeded gently up an energy channel that brought me closer to the radiant sun. I could feel myself being scanned and, in a strange way, instructed. I tried to convey my admiration and my understanding of the truly magnificent conversation that we were conducting. I felt tremendously excited, amused, energized and illuminated. Gradually I was tugged into a soft, creamy atmosphere, which electrified my body with pleasure. The closer I was pulled to the sun-surface the more I felt myself dissolving merging with the whirlpools of warm energy. Intense electric fingers strobed up-and-down my body which was turning itself inside out in acceptance. Strangely enough, at this moment of alleged "penetration" I felt like a vagina being turned inside out. The heat, light, power built up into a crescendo—and then to my utter delight I felt each atom of my being being embraced and linked up. With a soft-click I felt myself disintegrate into a total radiant union. As I felt the strong force take me over I heard Her voice murmur softly, *"I want you!"*

2

The Anxieties

I **recall eyeballing** with dreamy lasciviousness a 1936 *Saturday Evening Post* illustration of a young woman swinging on a hammock, her head tossed back in a gesture of innocent merriment, her white dress and lace petticoat pulled up, revealing two inches of milky, white, tender, moist, kissable inner thigh.

The year was 1938. Place: a small town in Western Massachusetts. Cultural background: Irish Catholic. Erotic climate: dry and frigid. Growing up in this chilly environment I was taught there was virtue and

Sex is the highest form of communication.

mortal sin—nothing in between. Good was to think and act like the neighbors, to be proper and decent. Bad? The human body. Any passing reference to sexual functions was very bad. The mention of genital organs was taboo! Erotic feelings—bad. Sexual desire—beyond bad. It was evil!

In my family, morality was administered by my mother and her two spinster sisters. As a youth I became aware of their strange obsession with sexuality. I watched with fascination as they scanned every work of art, every movie, every song, for any signs of what they referred to as "funny business". And it soon occurred to me—with genetic dismay—that my family, dominated by such anti-sex fervor, was dying out! Of my generation I was the only one to carry the paternal name and one of only two survivors on the maternal side.

This realization so disturbed me that I become determined to fight back. As the last remaining life form in my gene pool, I resolved that my family—and by extension, society's great Anti-Sex Gang—would not gain control over my precious bodily fluids. In short order, I managed to develop an equally sensitive counter-radar system that scanned every word and image in a fervent search for something—anything—mischievous, racy, erotic.

My first experience with erotic literature was provided by the Bible. I would sit pouring over Old Testament descriptions of lasciviousness, burningly aware of the fundamentalist erection bulging in my trousers while Mother and aunts beamed approval from the living room, sure that I would become a priest.

Soft-core porn abounded in the 1930s. Endlessly I eyeballed with dreamy lust the Montgomery Ward mail-order catalogue with its pictures of young trollops shamelessly modeling silken underwear. Pert wantons in nylon hose! Housewife harlots in steamy corsets. Vo-

Seven Styles in NYLON -- the Miracle Fabric

luptuous nymphomaniacs in one-piece bathing suits, crotch panels hugging tightly to the firm, labial curves. Sexual repression had created such a steamy hot-house atmosphere that the slightest spark could produce in me a pulsing flame.

Flashbackie:

Young Virginia Real, wearing a pressed convent school uniform, sits on one side of a confessional booth, twisting her flame-red hair.

"I let a boy feel my tits last night."

"Breasts," the priest on the other side corrects her. "Tits are vulgar."

"My breasts. First the left one. Then the right one. Then both together. Then just the left one again. Then—"

"You mustn't permit a representative of the devil to take advantage of your body, my child. That is a privilege which has to be *earned*."

"But why does God make it feel so nice then?"

"Allow me to quote from the Scriptures." He leafs through a Bible. "Here it is, the *Book of Job*. 'What? Shall we receive good at the hand of God, and shall we not receive evil? ' "

"I've read that too, Father, and it seems to me that God tosses out good and evil arbitrarily, just because Satan taunts him into it."

"God was testing Job's faith."

—Paul Krassner
Tales of Tongue Fu

This secret erotic library of my youth taught me a valuable lesson about the thermodynamics of sexual expression and repression. Sexual arousal is all in the mind. The human being comes equipped with sexual organs wired to the brain and booted up by hormones. The hardware is activated by various cues your brain has learned to associate with sexual invitations and availability. These cues, as shared by a particular society, become the pornography of that culture. Each society and each person develops unique trigger stimuli. The stimuli may change from person to culture to time frame. The girl in the hammock who was unbearably erotic to me in the 1950s would leave me yawning today. Even Jerry Falwell would rate the picture wholesome in the context of the 1980s.

But to someone else, in a personally or socially highly repressed environment, the innocent illustration may retain its tang of arousal. The sexual brain is wired to imprint as trigger stimuli any cue that turns you on. In this way, our brains always have the last laugh on the Anti-Sex Gang. The more that political or religious officials censor words and images about sex, the more suggestive and arousing becomes the lightest hint of double entendre, the slightest glimpse of a bodily part.

During the mid-1800s, women were "treated" with vibrators for what physicians called "hysteria." The word "hysteria" is derived from a Greek word meaning "suffering uterus." Women suffering from "hysteria" exhibited symptoms of anxiety, irritability, sexual fantasies, and "pelvic heaviness." To help alleviate these conditions, a physician would massage a patient's clitoris until "paroxysm"—orgasm—was achieved.

Or consider a photo of young men wrestling in Olympic competition, bodies locked and straining in muscular embrace. Such clean-cut, athletic activity could, for male homosexuals or certain horny, imaginative young women, became the porn trigger for hormone holocausts.

The prudish Arabs swathe their women in veils, and then writhe with lust at the sight of a bare ankle. Western feminists may wonder why their Islamic sisters put up with this male repression, but the veiled ladies are aware of the allure. I learned this in 1961 when Allen Ginsberg, William S. Burroughs, and I started flirting with a Moroccan singer in a Tangier café, and suddenly found ourselves being pulled into enormous, luscious nymphomaniac brown eyes as warm and melting as chocolate-pudding vaginas. I'm talking about two X-rated, hard-core eyeballs whose wet nakedness was demurely veiled by skillfully fluttering eyelids.

Those sexy Italians who grow and blossom in a Vatican-dominated black-robed repressive culture have developed an amazing shorthand for soft porn. Almost every fruit or vegetable, every household appliance—broom, rake, hammer, mop—is endowed with double meaning. Order a zucchini from the waiter in Naples, and a ripple of giggles goes around the table. Watch lusty Luigi hold a peach in his hot hand. Observe him slice it open, slowly, slowly. Watch him dreamily extract the stone, lovingly gaze into and then start to lick the pink-scarlet oval indentation! For Luigi, at that moment, no centerfold is as erotic as that hard-core, porno peach!

What is the sound of one hand clapping? The enthusiastic applause I receive after masturbating.
—Billy Shakespeare
The Complete Idiot's Guide
To Having Cybersex
With Other Complete Idiots

Pornography

PORNOGRAPHY, then, is whatever turns you on. The dictionary agrees. Pornography is defined as written, graphic, or
other forms of communication intended to excite sexual
desires. What could be clearer? Or healthier? I happen
to belong to that large percentage of human beings who
believe that sexual desire, being the undeniable source of
life, is sacred, and that when expressed by those whose
motives are reasonably healthy and loving, it creates the
highest form of human communication. And, to complete
this confessional, I have an innate, physical revulsion to violence. It disturbs me to look at films that involve fighting,
gunfire, bloodshed. The Rambo-type, to me, is a subhuman
monstrosity. Written or graphic expressions that stimulate
violent impulses—these are the true obscenities. And yet,
these are the expressions that are of no concern to the
anti-porn crusaders, the militaristic Hawks, the evangeli-
cal Rambos, the Thought Police, and the whole Anti-Sex
Gang. It is no coincidence: The
Anti-Sexers haven't the love or
the tenderness or the homi-
ness or the balls to appreciate
pornography. Violence or sex—
it's one or the other, it seems,
and I know where I stand. As
Mae West said to the guy with
the bulge in his trousers, "Is
that a gun in your pocket or are
you glad to see me?"

Mae West

In Search of the True Aphrodisiac

I want a new drug...

One that won't make me nervous,

wonderin' what to do...

One that makes me feel like I feel

when I'm with you.

—Huey Lewis and the News

At a very early age, after comparing the rather routine existence of my family with the heroic adventures I read about in books, I concluded that the well-lived life would necessarily involve quests. Grail adventures for fabled goals to save the human race.

During these younger years I dreamed of becoming a warrior, an explorer, a great scientist, a wise age. During adolescence a new noble challenge emerged: SEX.

Challenge of Sex

AND HERE I ENCOUNTERED a great and enduring paradox of the human condition—male division. To wit: Although sex was obviously important to a happy life, I did not have perfect control over my erections. Apparently many other males shared this inefficiency.

The first problem was that the erections came when I couldn't use them. The terrible embarrassment of the unexpected arousal in social situations. The inability to get up and walk across the room because of that mind-of-his-own down there.

Later came the nervousness of "making out". The wild excitement of foreplay. The unbuttoning of the bra. The removal of the panties. The wiggling into position in the front seat of the car. Would you believe a rumble seat? The zipper. The arrangement of the contraceptive. The heavy breathing. The anxieties. Do you hear someone coming? The maneuvering for penetration. When! What happened to my unit?

> How curious that such an important topic was totally ignored.

This interaction between the willing mind and the willful body suddenly became a most critical issue. And in puritanical 1936, there were no manuals on the care and use of this complex equipment.

I consulted the dictionary and discovered that something called an "aphrodisiac" increased sexual performance. I rushed to the library and consulted every encyclopedia available. Not a mention of aphrodisiac. How curious that such an important topic was totally ignored.

By 1950, sex was no problem. I was settled into the suburbs, happily married, and productively domesticated. My erections reported to duty promptly on schedule just as I did at the office.

3

QUEST FOR
THE MAGIC POTION

In **1960**, that magic year, I moved to Cambridge, Massachusetts, to join the Harvard faculty. My sexual situation was changed. I was a 40-year-old single person, facing, once again, the thrills, the chills, the spills of the mating ground. At this point I found that my sexuality (how shall I put this?) was very elitist and selective. I no longer felt that incessant, throbbing teenage desire to fuck any consenting warm body in the vicinity. A one-night stand could be a lust or a bust, depending on my feelings toward the woman, my emotional condition, my state of mind, and my period of heat.

To find out more about these matters, I read extensively on the subject and talked to my friends in the psychiatric, clinical, and personality departments. I learned that male sexuality is not an automatic macho scene. The male erotic response turned out to be a most complex, delicate situation. More than two-thirds of the male population over the age of 35 reported less than perfect control over their desire. Adult males seemed to have cycles and rhythm and all sorts of fragile sensitivities that are usually attributed to the "weaker sex". Scientific observers agreed that most of the guys who claimed total virility were either lying or too primitive and callous to appreciate the exquisite complications of erotic interaction in the fast-moving, ever-changing, postindustrial interactive civilization.

So here was an interesting social phenomenon. It was generally believed by psychologists back there in 1960 that much of the conflict, aggression, paranoia, and sadism that was plaguing society was due to sexual frustration. Freud started this line of thought. Wilhelm Reich carried it to its logical political conclusion. Sex means cheerfully giving up control to receive pleasure. The less sex, the more compulsion to control.

Take, for example, a control freak like J. Edgar Hoover. Here was a 70-year-old drag-queen who got his FBI kicks from collecting sexual dossiers on rival politicians. Or take, for example, Richard Nixon, whom no one ever accused of tender erotic feelings.

Wilhelm Reich

Wilhelm Reich was a psychoanalyst who focused on character structure, which put him at odds with his peers who viewed neurosis as the key. Reich alienated his peers by promoting teen sexuality, which for the 1930s and 40s was really out there. He went even further in promoting economic freedom for women, as well as availability of contraceptives and abortion.

Reich claimed that the link between human sexuality and neuroses, which he called "orgastic potency", is the foremost criterion for psycho-physical health. According to Reich sexual love depends on

Wilhelm Reich

one's ability to make love with "orgastic potency". He measured male orgasms, discovering four physiological phases: psychosexual tension; tumescence of the penis, orgasm, which includes an electrical discharge; and finally penis relaxation. He believed that this sexual force, which he called "orgone", is an energy present in all living things and the atmosphere itself.

Reich invented the "orgone accumulator" to harness orgone energy. As part of therapy his patients sat in the orgone box. The psychoanalytic establishment denounced this work and called him as mentally ill. Reich often had his patients strip down to their underwear during psychoanalysis—men in boxers and women in bra and panties. If that were bad enough, Reich often used touch in his session to feel the patient's breathing or to reposition their bodies.

These many breeches of analytical taboos enraged the psychoanalytic community who declared him insane. In the late 1940s the Food and Drug Administration (FDA) launched an investigation into Reich's claims about orgone and the Court enjoined him from selling his orgone boxes across state lines. Reich ignored them—of course—promptly violated the injunction and was charged with contempt of court. Refusing all legal advice, he carried on his own defense, arguing that matters of science are not decided in the court room. He lost and was sentenced to two years behind bars.

Books containing the forbidden word "orgone" were ordered destroyed. In August 1956, the FDA burned tons of writing in garbage incinerator.

Just as he was eligible for parole, Reich died from heart failure in the Lewisburg, Pennsylvania federal penitentiary on November 18, 1957. No psychiatric or scientific journal carried an obituary. The rest of the psychoanalytic community learned what happens when they stray from the hive.

Orgone

Orgone was discovered by Wilheim Reich, whose research showed that orgone energy fills all space, expands and contracts in pulsatory rhythm. All matter attracts orgone, but at different rates of speed. Water strongly attracts the orgone, or life-energy, giving rise to the phenomenon of living water (described classically as "activated" or "structured" water) which is fundamental to life processes, and to the Earth's weather as well.

Reich invented a special metal-lined enclosure to attract orgone energy from the atmosphere into a box he called the orgone en-

Man in orgone box

ergy accumulator. His experiments showed that the orgone box could charge seeds and increase plant growth, speed the healing of burns and cuts. Reich believed Reich that illnesses like cancer were low-energy problems that could be helped with orgone.

Supporters believe that Reich's experiments held promise for new methods to end drought and green deserts, detoxify nuclear waste—even provide a pollution-free energy that can propel rocket ships through space.

J. Edgar Hoover
FBI Director

Hoover was a lifelong bachelor, and since at least the 1940s unsubstantiated rumors have circulated that he was homosexual and that Clyde Tolson, associate director of FBI was his lover because the two men were virtually inseparable. They worked together all day, shared most meals, frequently were seen together in trendy night clubs, and vacationed together.

Tolson accepted the American flag that draped Hoover's casket, inherited Hoover's estate and moved into his home. He is buried near Hoover in the Congressional Cemetery.

Countless rumors say Hoover loved to "dress up" in women's clothes—then he became a she, named J. Edna Hoover. Susan Rosenstiel was quoted in The Secret Life of J. Edgar Hoover by Anthony Summers saying she saw him in a fluffy black dress with lace, stockings, high heels and a black curly wig.

Hoover is reputed to have conducted surveillance on Eleanor Roosevelt with alleged lesbian lovers—presumably in case black mail became necessary. It is also widely believed that he planted rumors that Adlai Stevenson was gay to hurt his Presidential Campaign. Many claim Hoover is the poster child

J. Edgar Hoover

for homophobia as evidenced by his persecution of homosexuals while he himself engaged in homosexuality and transvestism.

4

Taboo

In the spring of 1960, I concluded that if a safe, dependable aphrodisiac were available, many of the psychological and social problems facing our society would instantly be ameliorated. So I descended on the Harvard Medical School library with a team of graduate assistants. We scoured the bibliographies and journal files for data about aphrodisiac drugs and discovered an enormous literature on the subject.

Oh well, here was another unexplained, mysterious facet of adult life. Lindbergh could fly the Atlantic. We could put a man on the South Pole. But we couldn't get control of the most important part of our body. Maybe this was what philosophers meant by the "mind/body problem." I resolved to file this away for future study.

The mandrake root was apparently the first sex stimulus. It was mentioned twice in the *Bible*. Pythagoras "advocated" it. Machiavelli wrote a comedy about it.

Mandrake

Mandrake belongs to the nightshades family and related to Belladonna. The roots resemble human figures and contain the hallucinogenic tropane alkaloids.

Mandrake was used in magic rituals in antiquity and is still used neopagan religions such as Wicca. Reports show that magicians formed it into a resemblance of the human figure.

In the old Herbals Mandrake is shown as a male with a long beard, and a female with a very bushy head of hair. There are weird superstitions surrounding the root. As an amulet, it was placed on mantelpieces to avert misfortune and to bring prosperity and happiness to the house.

The flesh and organs of horny animals had been used in almost every time and place. Hippomanes, flesh from the forehead of a colt, was mentioned in Virgil. Mediaeval Europeans regularly used the penis of a stag, bull, ox, goat.

But most frequent in the depictions is the dancing to the music of the flute, always the maddening hissing sound of the double flute, with their heads thrown back in indication of their ecstatic state. They dance, moreover, with satyrs, the goat-men, who can only be creatures from a metaphysical realm, beyond the ordered cosmos. Apart from being grossly ithyphallic, they represent the recidivist forces, a return to the times of female dominance, for the penis is obviously beyond a man's conscious control when the beauty of the female magically induces its lustful arousal. The phallus alone represents this aspect of the god. The goat, moreover, demonstrated itself as the culti-

Throughout the ages, intelligent, affluent, ambitious, and just plain horny human beings have continually sought the alchemical grail-the true aphrodisiac.

vated god's enemy as being only too eager to graze upon the vineyards. Goats, moreover, will graze on everything, often indicating to the herdsman the psychoactive potential of certain wild herbs by their effect upon his herd. By one account, it was a goat grazing on the vine that led to the discovery of wine.

These goat men cavort sexually with the maenads. The women can themselves become goats, wearing a goatskin around their waist, and dancing as they expose their breasts to view, like the Minoan herbalists, clearly female, but displaying a penis as well, appended to their goat masquerade. They are all the god's nymphs, which means simply his "brides'" for the god, too, was apt to materialize in his various forms amidst their revels, dancing with them, disguising, what in his troupe of satyrs could not be hidden, namely his own virulent maleness by a masquerading dress, despite his beard, as a fellow female, sharing in the coven of the sisterhood liberated in the hunt. The cross-dressing of both the women and the god is indicative of their perfect sexual harmony.

But the god is also a bull, and although he himself is never depicted ithyphallic, like the satyrs, the erection beneath the disguise of dress can materialize as a priapic idol, representing the son he begot upon the goddess Aphrodite.

—Carl Ruck
Sacred Mushrooms of the Goddess
Secrets of Eleusis

Ambergris, a jelly from the innards of the whale, was used by the royal mistress Madame du Barry and the insatiably curious James Boswell. Musk was a perennial favorite of erotic searchers; so was shellfish, of course, especially oysters and mussels. In Japan, the firgu fish, a form of puffer, is still used by hopeful lovers. Each year more than five hundred Japanese die while on this dangerous quest.

All the texts agreed that cantharides, Spanish Fly, is a "most certain and terrible aphrodisiac." An overdose causes unbearable itching and irritation to the genitals.

Spanish Fly

The Spanish fly is a emerald green blister beetle found in the southern parts of Europe. The dried and crushed body of the Spanish Fly beetle is regarded as a potent aphrodisiac for hundreds of years. The liquid irritates the urogenital tract and produces an itching sensation in sensitive membranes, a feeling that is believed to increase a woman's desire for intercourse.

Over the centuries the plant kingdom has been ransacked by the sexually ambitious. Many believe that satyrian, a mythic herb mentioned by the Greeks and Romans, was nothing else than good old marijuana and hashish. Then there's truffles and mushrooms. The South American yage. The South Seas root kava kava. Damiana. The royal jelly and pollen from bees.

And, of course, the coca plant. Pre-Columbian Peruvian ceramics portrayed pornographic scenes on pots used to prepare the nose candy of the Andes. Is cocaine an aphrodisiac? "First you're hot and then you're not," reported most sophisticated researchers.

Casanova attributed his record-making lust to raw eggs.

The strong, hard, up-jutting horn of the rhino has caught the imagination of erection-seekers for centuries. You grind it up into powder and eat or toot it. In the Orient, rhino dust goes for $2,000 an ounce. In Hong Kong restaurants they'll sprinkle some rhino-horn powder on your dinner for a hefty addition to your bill.

My research at the Harvard Medical School library thus demonstrated that my quest was not a lonely one. Throughout the ages, intelligent, affluent, ambitious, and just plain horny human beings have continually sought the alchemical grail—the true aphrodisiac.

So what does modern science have to contribute to this noble search? Nothing. Nada. Zilch.

Not only was there no proven aphrodisiac in the current medical literature, there was apparently no research being done on this most important topic. How curious. Here was a medicine that could cure many of our medical and psychological problems, and there seemed to be a veil of secrecy around the subject.

A Taboo Subject

WHEN I TRIED TO TALK TO MY FRIENDS on the medical faculty about this subject, they clammed up. Finally an endocrinologist pal explained it to me. "Listen, Timothy, the subject of aphrodisiacs is taboo. If any medical scientist or physiologist here, or in the Soviet Union, were to apply for a grant to research this field, his reputation would be ruined. He'd be considered a flake."

"But it's a great research topic," I protested. "The first scientist who discovers an effective aphrodisiac will be a savior of mankind and make a bundle of money."

"No question of it," said the endocrinologist "We all know that if a crack team of psychopharmacologists were to research this topic, they could come up with an aphrodisiac in a year. It will happen. Someday someone will win a Nobel prize and make a billion dollars marketing one. But this is only 1958. Eisenhower is president; Khrushchev is premier. There's an overpopulation problem. The culture isn't ready for a medicine that would have the male population running around with erect dicks bulging out of their pants. Jeez, we're just coming up with a polio vaccine. Come back in twenty years, and maybe we'll have an erection injection."

There was no doubt about it. There was a social taboo against the idea of a pill that would give man a calm, certain control over his precious equipment. I couldn't understand it, if your car decided to run when it wanted to, you'd have it adjusted right away. If your television set was temperamental and turned off at its own whim, you'd take steps to put you back in charge.

This resistance to self-improvement became really obvious when I was taken to see a sex show in the Reeperbahn of Hamburg, Germany. My guides were a very sophisticated editor of Der Speigel and a well-known psychiatrist. The show amazed me. Straight-out fucking on stage! I was most impressed by a big Swedish youth who bounded around the set with this enormous hard-on, fucking first this fiery red-head who wrapped her legs around him, and then a sultry brunette who lay on a couch holding up her arms invitingly, and then pleasuring the saucy blonde who bent over, leaning her head against the wall with her backsides wiggling.

For twenty minutes this acrobatic young man pranced around with total self-mastery in front of an audience of two hundred! We're talking Olympic gold-medal time!

"That guy's stamina is impressive," I said to my German hosts. They scoffed in that scornful, jaded Hamburg style.

"That's not the real thing," said the editor. "He's taken some drug."

The psychiatrist agreed, waving his hand in dismissal.

I leaped to my feet. "What drug!" I shouted. "What's it called? Where can you get it?"

No answer from my sophisticated friends. They just couldn't admit to being interested.

Kind of Union

MAN is divided into three classes, viz. the hare man, the bull man, and the horse man, according to the size of his lingam.

Woman also, according to the depth of her yoni, is either a female deer, a mare, or a female elephant.

In these unequal unions, when the male exceeds the female in point of size, his union with a woman who is immediately next to him in size is called high union, and is of two kinds; while his union with the woman most remote from his size is called the highest union, and is of one kind only. On the other hand, when the female exceeds the male in point of size, her union with a man immediately next to her in size is called low union, and is of two kinds; while her union with a man most remote from her in size is called the lowest union, and is of one kind only.

In other words, the horse and mare, the bull and deer, form the high union, while the horse and deer form the highest union. On the female side, the elephant and bull, the mare and hare, form low unions, while the elephant  has and the hare make the lowest unions. There are, then, nine kinds of union according to dimensions. Amongst all these, equal unions are the best, those of a superlative degree, i.e. the highest and the lowest, are the worst, and the rest are middling, and with them the high are better than the low.

—Mallanaga Vatsyayana
Kamasutra

5

Aphrodisiacs

Aphrodite, the Greek goddess of sexual love and beauty, rose out of the sea on an oyster shell to give birth to Eros—the god of love, sexuality and fertility. An aphrodisiac is a drug, herb, potion, food or other scent that stimulates sexual desire.

Oysters are claimed to have aphrodisiac qualities, but science has not verified the aphrodisiac qualities of oysters. Scientists say that sexual desire is all in the mind—if you think something is an aphrodisiac, it is for you.

Foods that resemble human genitalia, like bananas, cucumbers, and seafood like oysters and mussels, are often believed to have sexual powers. Essential oil like ylang-ylang and some herbs can have an effect on the nervous system, producing calming, euphoric feelings that soothe negativity and stress, promoting intimacy and relaxation.

Aphrodite rising out of the sea on an oyster shell.

Anchovies, Spanish fly, lard, and licorice are thought to have erotic-inducing qualities. The definition of aphrodisiac requires the substance to normally produce an increase in sexual desire, so alcohol is not considered an aphrodisiac. There are hundreds, if not thousands, of claimed aphrodisiacs, and science reckons they are all folklore, despite large numbers of us still trying to find the magic potion, lotion or pill to increase and improve our sex lives.

Rhino horn is sometimes thought to be an aphrodisiac because of its phallic shape, but in fact the horn is eaten to increase libido. The horn contains mostly phosphorus and calcium, which, if ingested, may increase health in a person previously lacking in these, and may therefore increase sexual responses.

Luv-Mu-Tea

For Increased Sexual Energy

Calamus (broken	1 oz.
Muira Puama (shaved)	2 oz.
Ginseng (broken)	1 oz.
Vanilla Pods (chopped)	3 pods
Kola Nuts (broken)	2 oz.
Betel Nuts (broken)	1/2 oz.
Southernwood (shaved)	1 oz.
Yohimbe Bark (shaved)	1 oz.
Nutmeg (broken)	2 nuts
Cloves (whole)	1/2 oz.

The ingredients are combined homogeneously and stored in a sealed container under refrigeration. 1/2 oz. is boiled for 5-10 minutes in a 4-cup pyrex®

coffeemaker. One or more cups are drunk one hour before intercourse. A second and possibly third pot may be prepared by adding fresh water to be remaining pulp and boiling for slightly longer periods.

—Adam Gottlieb
Sex Drugs and Aphrodisiacs

Popular Aphrodisiacs

ABSINTHIUM was a green colored tonic used by sophisticated ladies in the 1880s. It is extracted from wormwood and contains many toxic compounds. With habitual use can cause nerve problems, blindness, and abdominal cramp and was outlawed in France in 1915 and continues to be banned in most European countries.

Ambergris is a solid waxy substance originating in the intestine of the sperm whale. In the West it was used as a fixative for rare perfumes since it has the effect of making fragrances last much longer than they would otherwise. The notion that certain scents can stimulate erotic feelings is the basic for using perfumes.

Amphetamines, or "speed", can increase libido and sexual pleasure in low doses taken orally. Even at moderate doses, however, impotence becomes more common in men, with decreased libido occurring in both sexes. At high doses, some intravenous amphetamine users reported experiencing "pharmacogenic orgasm,"—a drug-generated orgasm that has nothing to do with sexual intercourse.

Amyl Nitrate or "poppers" were popular as a recreational drug in the late 1970s. People use poppers as a way to heighten the sensations experienced during sex—especially orgasm. It works by reducing blood pressure to cause heightening awareness, altering mood, and causing dizziness. Inhaling amyl nitrate vapor can cause hemolysis—destruction of red blood cells, and methemoglobinemia—conversion of hemoglobin into a chemical that cannot carry oxygen.

Bremelanotide is used in an inhaler and some believe it is the long-sought female version of Viagra®. Bremelanotide stimulates the brain, rather than the genitals. It was originally developed for use in treating sexual dysfunction but this application was discontinued in 2008, after concern about adverse side effects of increased blood pressure.

Bull Penis, under the law of similarity, is believed to increase sexual stamina and potency. Other popular penis include Goat Penis, Horse Penis, Ox Penis, Stag Penis.

Coca is the plant from which cocaine is synthesized. People who chew coca leaves eat less and have stamina, which may prolong intercourse.

Cocaine often has the reverse effect, increasing sexual desire while impairing or delaying orgasm. However, a symptom of heavy cocaine abuse is a massive decline in sex drive and activity.

Cordyceps was used as an aphrodisiac and anti-aging tonic by the Emperor and his court. Cordyceps is a fungus found growing on dead caterpillars. It is possible to cultivate the mycelia and grow it on sterilized grain, or in vats of nutrient broth the way yeast is grown.

Crocin is the chemical ingredient primarily responsible for the color of saffron and for its libido-boosting power. The role of two major saffron chemicals (crocin and safranal) was investigated and it was shown that crocin had major effects on sexual behavior, while safranal had essentially none. male mice given crocin had an increase in erections, mounting attempts and ejaculation

Dark Chocolate. Women who eat chocolate regularly have higher levels of sexual desire than women who don't indulge. Chocolate contains phenyl-ethylamine, which stimulates the release of dopamine into the pleasure centers commonly associated with an orgasm. Women who consume large quantities of chocolate have more satisfying sex lives.

DHEA is a steroid produced by the adrenal glands, the gonads, and other cells in the body. DHEA is required for making testosterone and estrogen. DHEA is available as a supplement in the U.S. and is widely considered an aphrodisiac. There are many reports of DHEA stoking the fires of passion. Five mg. daily has a libido boosting effect. Men report frequent spontaneous erections, more vivid fantasies, and more drive in the bedroom.

Ecstacy (MDMA) is known as the "love drug" because it causes all-encompassing feelings of affection, euphoria, and heightened sensitivity in some people. Related to amphetamines and the hallucinogen mescaline, Ecstasy has been shown to have potentially neurotoxic effects on serotonin, causing, among other problems, abnormal regrowth of the nerves that produce it.

Fugu Fish, or Puffer Fish, describes several related species of fish that are consumed in Japan and Korea. Puffer fish contains a powerful poison, and people die every year from consuming it. Yet people pay hundreds of dollars per plate. Enthusiasts claim that a non-lethal dose of puffer fish toxin is a powerful stimulant and aphrodisiac. It causes tingling in the lips, fingers, and toes, and penis. It is also a nerve poison that increases stiffness of the muscles.

Ginkgo Biloba is a treatment for antidepressant-induced sexual dysfunction. It boosts blood flow to the genitals. People with low sex drive is linked with mental fatigue, poor memory, stress during times of intensive study, peripheral vascular disease or cold extremities, and smokers report firmer erections. Men at their sexual prime who take antidepressant medication common face loss of libido and have erectile difficulties.

Ginseng is used in China as a sexual balancer and a supplement to maintaining health balance of an individual. It boosts energy, including sex drive, and supports the immune system. It also helps a person adapt to physical or emotional stress and fatigue. Ginseng also has a normalizing effect on people going through the discomforts of hormone imbalances; it boosts metabolic rate and improves blood flow to the genitals. Ginseng promotes natural and increased testosterone levels in the body, as well as the number and motility of sperm cells.

Goji Berry is a well regarded aphrodisiac food in China, where it is referred to as the "happy berry". Goji is considered a yin tonic, and strengthens the liver and the kidney/adrenal system, which is believed to be the source of sexual energy in Chinese medicine.

Hashish and Marijuana initially increase libido and potency, but chronic use causes sexual inversion. Smoking may encourage sexual excitation through disinhibition.

Hippomanes is the slime of sexually aroused mare. It forms in the cavity of the placenta where the fetus was located.

The member of Abu'l-Haylukh remained
In erection for 30 days, sustained
By smoking hashish.
Abu'l-Hayluk deflowered in one night
Eighty virgins in a rigid rite
After smoking hashish –
Or so the legend goes.

Horny Goat Weed acts by inhibiting the PDE-5 enzyme, which is the same way that the popular drug Viagra® works. Some evidence suggests horny goat weed may modulate levels of the hormones cortisol, testosterone, and thyroid hormone, bringing low levels back to normal. The soft green heart-shaped leaf of the horny goat weed could hold the key to a new drug for treating erectile dysfunction because it has testosterone-like effects, stimulating sexual desire, sperm production, and stimulates sensory nerves.

Kava Kava causes sedation, and in high amounts, intoxication, Kava soothes anxiety. The main active components in kava root are called kavalactones, which may affect the levels of neurotransmitters—chemicals that carry messages from nerve cells to other cells. Kava affects the levels of specific neurotransmitters, including norepinephrine, gamma aminobutyric acid (GABA) and dopamine.

Mandrake Root. Magically speaking, the female mandrake root is forked and looks like a pair of human legs, whereas the male has only a single root. It is associated with fertility and is the most powerful herb of love magick. It is also one of the most deadliest. Roots that resemble a phallus are believed to possess great aphrodisiac qualities Both male and female fertility is promoted by eating mandrake—males eat the male mandrake root and females eat the female mandrake root—or by carrying one as a charm, according to legend. A tiny particle of powdered female mandrake leaf is added to a cup of red wine for passionate lovemaking or to white wine for romantic love and said to be a powerful Witch's aphrodisiac.

Melanotan is considered a potential treatment for sexual dysfunction. Developed as a skin tanning agent, users discovered that it stimulates desire and makes the penis more rigid.

Oysters, Clams and Mussels contain compounds that have been shown to be effective in releasing sexual hormones such as testosterone and estrogen. To feel sexy include at least a quarter cup of mussels or four medium-sized oysters or clams in your diet every week.

Oysters are believed to be an aphrodisiac.

Beware of red tide warnings, however. Bivalve shellfish can be extremely poisonous when it originates from affected areas. Casanova ate dozens every morning according to legend.

Many believe that Zinc holds the explanation for oysters' ability to boost libido. A deficiency of zinc can limit testosterone production in the body, and oysters are loaded with zinc. Iodine, another chemical element found in oysters, is essential for thyroid hormone production, and in some people, a moderate dose of iodine can give a noticeable boost to respiration, body temperature, and physical activity.

p-Chlorophenylalanine (PCPA) has is a popular sexual stimulant because it inhibits or reduces the production of serotonin, a powerful vasoconstrictor (i.e., it reduces blood flow), thereby increasing sexual desire.

Phenylethylamine (PEA) generates a mild, positive effect of phentolamine across all measures of arousal, with significant changes in self-reported lubrication and pleasurable sensations in the vagina.

Rhinoceros Horn contains ethanolamine, phosphorous, and sugar, along with the free amino acids threonine, aspartic acid, lysine, histidine, ornithine, and arginine. This last ingredient has a reputation for raising the intensity of sexual sensation, although there is little evidence to support this assertion. Rhino horn is made of keratin—the same material of which our nails and hair is made.

Spanish fly: As the story goes, in 1752 a Frenchman was prescribed 2 drams of cantharides for a fever and in the next two months bedded his wife at least 87 times. Another man with a similar prescription "knew his wife", as the Bible puts it, 40 times in one night. Cantharides is a dangerous toxin—one thousandth of an ounce of the active chemical in cantharides is sufficient to cause kidney failure and death. It is illegal worldwide.

Testosterone is a proven aphrodisiac. It is not The Perfect Aphrodisiac that solves all sexual problems, but it generally increases libido, and can have dramatic effects in some people. Natural testosterone boosters include: Exercise, Zinc, and Boron. Although testosterone is thought of as a male hormone, both men and women produce it. While women have lower amounts, but it definitely affects their sexual metabolism.

> The brain is the ultimate organ of pleasure.

Truffles: There are two kinds of truffles. One kind is an aphrodisiac mushroom that looks like a rock or gnarly potato; the other is a chocolate candy made to look like something like a mushroom truffle. The essence is strong, and a little goes a long way. Truffles are a food like caviar or chilies.

Wild Lettuce (Lactuca virosa). The ancient Egyptians purportedly possessed a book of love agents that contained recipes for aphrodisiacs, many of which were said to made

What happened to the good old-fashioned orgy?

with the lactucarium of wild lettuce. The book is lost, but references are found in ancient texts. Ancient Greeks believed that wild lettuce promoted the menses cycle, as well as decreased the libido and inhibited coitus.

Yohimbe comes from the bark of an African tree. It stimulates the nerve centers in the spine that control erection.

6

Aphrodisiac Effect of Psychedelic Drugs

I n August 1960, beside a swimming pool in Mexico, I ate psilocybin mushrooms and discovered the power of psychedelic drugs to program the brain.

I rushed back to Harvard. Frank Barron and I started the Harvard Psychedelic Drug Research project Aldous Huxley and Alan Watts and Allen Ginsberg were our advisors. We assembled thirty of the brightest young researchers in the area. We were on to something that could change human nature. We felt like Oppenheimer after his Almagordo bomb, except better, because psychedelic drugs allowed you to release the nuclear energies inside your own head.

In the next two years the Harvard Psychedelic Drug Research project studied the reactions of a thousand subjects to LSD. We discovered that the key to a psychedelic drug session is set and setting.

Set is your mind fix. Your psychological state. Be very careful what you want from a session, because you're likely to get it.

Setting is the environment. If your surroundings are scary, then you'll be scared. If your surroundings are beautiful, then you'll have a beautiful experience.

Our sessions at Harvard were designed for self-discovery. The sessions were held in groups. So neither the set nor the setting emphasized sex.

My colleague Richard Alpert, who later became the famous holy man Baba Ram Dass, was much more hip. He quickly discovered that if the set—and expectation—was erotic, and the setting was his bedroom, then psychedelic drugs were powerfully aphrodisiac. I give the wily Ram Dass a lot of credit for this breakthrough. He was certainly way ahead of me.

I remember the day he came to me and said, "All this inner exploration stuff is great. It's true you can access any circuit in your brain and change your mind. But it's time you faced the facts, Timothy. We're turning on the most powerful sexual organ in the universe! The brain."

Other sophisticated people came to Harvard and tipped us to the secret. The philosopher Gerald Heard. The beat poet Allen Ginsberg. The Buddhist sage Alan Watts. The western folk hero Neil Cassady. We were just rediscovering what philosophers and poets and mystics and musicians and hedonists had known for centuries. Marijuana,

> All this inner exploration stuff is great. It's true you can access any circuit in your brain and change your mind. But it's time you faced the facts, Timothy. We're turning on the most powerful sexual organ in the universe! The brain.
> —Baba Ram Dass

The effect was in the head. If you knew how to dial and tune your brain, you could enrich your sex life beyond your wildest dreams.

hashish, mushrooms, LSD were powerful sensory experiences.

For the next twenty years, like everyone else, I multiplied my sensory pleasure, learned the techniques of erotic engineering. Everything became a source of aesthetic-erotic pleasure, etc. The effect was in the head. If you knew how to dial and tune your brain, you could enrich your sex life beyond your wildest dreams.

But there was still that matter of controlling the rod of flesh. We could boogie around in our brains. Good! But why couldn't a man be able to operate his penis at will the way he moves the voluntary organs of his body?

Sex, Ecstasy & Psychedelic Drugs

When two people are longtime lovers, they may feel, in the psychedelic drug state, an emotional closeness as intense as they felt in the early, most emotion-charged stages of being in love. Since visual perception is highly responsive to the emotions, each partner may take on an appearance of extraordinary radiance and beauty. Communication may seem multileveled, with a greatly heightened sensitivity to nuances of meaning - in gestures, caresses and words as well. If this couple decides to make love, they will bring this heightened sensitivity to their union, and their desire and the act itself may be suffocated with the same positive emotion - and with the same beauty - that has been present in their perceptions....

The sexual union gathers ever more meaning and beauty as it progresses. It may even take on symbolic and archetypal overtones. The couple may feel that they are mythic, legendary, or more-than-human figures as they act out in a timeless and beneficent space of eternally recurring drama of love and creation. The feeling of being more than human does not indicate grandiosity but, rather, that one has transcended the ordinary boundaries of self, the limits of time and space, so that something more, some infusion of the divine or supernatural, must have occurred. This awareness is accompanied by profound feelings of security, tenderness, humility and gratitude. Sometimes only one partner will enjoy this transcendental experience, but with surprising frequency the feelings are shared.

When sexual union includes altered states of consciousness such as these, it is properly described as ecstatic....

The orgasm, too, is 'psychedelic' - that is, magnified or intensified. Time distortion can greatly prolong it, and there is an awareness of the whole process from beginning to end, in far greater detail.

— R.E.L. Masters

Pete Von Sholly

7

Brain Sex Multiplies RPMs

(Raptures Per Minute)

The major scientific-political issues of the 1960s involved control of the Automobile Body for individual pleasure* Freedom to use neurosomatic and brain-reward drugs, sexual freedom, freedom of dress and grooming, refusal to have one's body used as a military instrument or as an economic tool. The Adult Authorities in almost every National Hive also use Fifth Circuit sensory stimuli to torture and coerce. Rapture and torture thus became neuro-political issues. In general, countries that allowed rapture prohibited torture, and vice-versus.

It is of interest that humanity's first inter-planetary mission was named "Apollo," honoring the Roman-Greek God. Apollo II, Leo II are pre-scientific labels for the neuro-genetic caste that links the neur-electric and atom energies necessary to crate new post-terrestrial hives.

See it, feel it, smell it, shape it—with your mind.

Telepathic Fusion is the neurological equivalent of the linkage of two self-actualized bodies to activate neuro-electric consciousness. In this case two or more self-actualized Brains fuse and activate RNA-DNA consciousness.

Brain-sex produces genetic consciousness and opens the way to Egg-Intelligence.

Just as two Tantric lovers can create new-rological realities—so do two brain mates form new RNA-DNA realities.

Tantric Union

TANTRA IS A YOGIC TECHNIQUE in which the totality of one's erotic potential is fused in union with a member of the opposite sex. Such a synergic union harmonizes all the neurosomatic energies and makes possible the next step in evolution: Brain Control.

By 1979 the production of somatic-electricity between the two self-actualized Hedonists was as obvious—and to the uninitiated, as mysterious—as Benjamin Franklin's experimental summoning down of lightening bolts. The experiments can be easily replicated at home.

1. Retire to a comfortable bedroom where there is total privacy.

2. Ingest an adequate amount of a neurosomatic drug. The amount and the name of this neuro-transmitter varies from niche-to-niche and from brain to brain. Such drugs have, at times, been called MDA, X.T.C.

3. Arrange the two naked bodies in any standard fact-to-face tantric attitude—legs intertwined, woman's yoni above man' lingam.

4. The two experimenters then softly stroke each other's bodies for at least an hour. The soft friction of the two aroused skin surfaces then produces an electrical aura. This usually appears first on the hands—often seen as film-like grids between the fingers. Or as loose "rubber-glove-like" auras sound the fingers. The grids are clearly electromagnetic structures in that objects can be passed through them. But they can be manipulated by moving the electrically-charged finger close to them. The magnetic attraction is often visible as thread-like filaments growing up from the arms. Tiny threads emitted from certain marine forms, such as Portugese men or war, for example, which contain at the ends electrical charges. The charges in this case are pleasurable rather than defensive.

The production of such magnetic auras indicated that the neuro-electric circuit is being activated.

Wonderful, Sexy Neurotransmitters!

When social psychologist Arthur Aron scanned the brains of young people looking at a photo of persons they said they were madly in love, the brain areas that "lit up" were those rich in a powerful "feel good" chemical, dopamine. Dopamine plays a big role in the excitement of love and is the key chemical in the brain's "reward system," a network of cells associated with pleasure.

When Aron scanned the brains of older couples, who claimed to still be intensely in love after two decades of marriage, the same brain areas lit up. Interestingly, other areas of the brain also lit up in these folks—those rich in oxytocin.

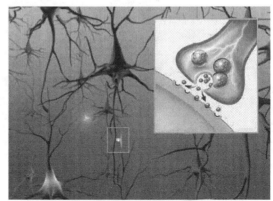

Oxytocin, often called the "cuddling" chemical, is a mammalian hormone

The neurotransmitters travel across the synapse, carrying signals to other cells.

that also acts as a neurotransmitter in the brain. It helps new mothers make milk and bond with their babies, is secreted by both sexes during orgasm, and has been linked in animals to monogamy and long-term attachment. Because oxytocin is released in men and women during sexual orgasm, it may be involved in adult bonding. Interestingly, both Prozac, an antidepressant, and Viagra®, an erection enhancer, appear to affect the oxytocin system.

The spirit is willing, but the flesh is weak. But if you keep licking me there, I guarantee the flesh will catch up pretty quick.
—Billy Shakespeare
The Complete Idiot's Guide
To Having Cybersex
With Other Complete Idiots

8

Encounter with
Medical Science

One night in 1983, I was having dinner with a friend who worked at the UCLA Neuropsychiatric Institute. During the evening, he mentioned that a breakthrough in the erection department was at hand. He said that a Stanford University research team was developing a pill that would give immediate control of your erections! The active ingredient was called *yohimbe*.

This was a discovery of historic importance! It could mean the end of male insecurity, cruelty, and war! This could break the wretched addiction to prime-time television!

Yohimbine

Yohimbine is a tryptamine alkaloid found in Pausinystalia yohimbe or yohimbe bark. It is a stimulant and believed to have aphrodisiac qualities. Medical studies in humans have shown yohimbine to be effective in the treatment of male impotence.

Erectile dysfunction has been treated with Yohimbine Hydrochloride, USP—a prescription medicine. However studies show that the treatment for
impotence is not always effective since there can be
many causes of impotence. Although many insist
that it does increase libido, but this has not been
supported by research.

Yohimbine has been found to relax and dilate
blood vessels in the penis, resulting in increased
blood flow and erection. It may also stimulate areas
in the brain involved in sexual desire.

Yohimbine can cause anxiety reactions, such as
rapid heart rate, high blood pressure, overstimula-
tion, insomnia and/or sleeplessness, and can be
dangerous if used in high doses. There have been
reports of panic attacks, hallucinations, headaches,
dizziness, and skin flushing—even seizures and renal
failure.

My friend also said that a local group, the Southern California Sexual Dysfunction Clinic, was giving these new pills
to research subjects. I phoned and made an appointment
with the director. If the pill existed, I wanted to try it out,
and help make it available to the public.

The clinic was in the Cedar Sinai Medical Center. There
was a large waiting room. About eight very old men were
sitting slumped over, staring glumly at the carpet. A couple had crutches.

Two old geezers were drooling.

The nurse greeted me cordially and asked me to fill out
a form. I said, "I'm here to discuss research on aphrodisiacs
with the doctor." She smiled compassionately and said she
understood, but would I please fill out the forms. So I did.

After a while a male technician, about 40, with the graceful charm of a chic hair-dresser, asked me to come to a back room. I explained that I wanted to discuss research with the doctor. He smiled understandingly and asked me to take some tests. At this point I was about to say "forget it," but it occurred to me that this would be a great opportunity see what happens in these frontiers of medical science. And I realized that the doctor wasn't going to give me pills until I had taken the tests.

So I took the standard blood and urine tests.

Then came the mad-scientist stuff. The technician patiently explained that we had to find out if there was a strong and steady flow of blood to my unit. So he wired the tip of my module, the back of my module, and an artery in my leg to an amplifier and we sat back to listen. BOOM ... BOOM ... BOOM! My genital bloodstream filled the room with its strong stallion pulse! Sounded like the rhythm section of a heavy-metal rock group to me.

The technician nodded in approval.

Next he had me jog in place, my unit still wired for sound. The percussion section rally took off. Boom ... da ... BOOM!

All the time I kept explaining that I had regular, if unpredictable erections. I just wanted the pill! The technician was very understanding. "Tell it to the doctor," he said.

The doc was very cordial and understanding. He evaded my questions about the aphrodisiac. He explained how complicated this field was—the mind, the brain, the hormones, the circulatory system, phobias, repressions, venereal diseases, herpes, AIDS, alcohol and drug abuse, fatigue, overwork, marital discord, inherited dispositions, early traumas, fetishes, anxieties, menopausal life stages.

At this point it dawned on me that this clinic, supposedly set up to deal with sexual arousal, was the most antiseptic, mechanical, unerotic place I had ever encountered. I could feel my reservoir of sexual desire rapidly draining away. If I didn't have an erection problem before, I was very likely to catch one in here. This place could make Casanova take a vow of chastity.

I felt like the ambitious starlet who undressed for the producer, the casting director, the script writer, the director, the director's brother Max, and won a part in a safari movie that required her to live in a tent on the wind-swept, dismal Sahara desert. "Who do I have to fuck to get out of this sexual-dysfunction movie?" I thought to myself.

The doctor was relentless. He insisted that I take the erection-frequency test. You took the gadget home and wired up your module during sleep to measure the number and strength of nocturnal hard-ons. I explained that I had them all the time. "Listen, just phone my wife. She takes Richterscale readings every night"

The male nurse outfitted me with the peter-meter, stored for travel in a large suitcase. All the old men in the waiting room looked up sadly as I bounced by with the case.

My wife was intrigued. She couldn't wait for me to try it. We rushed to the bedroom and set it up by the side of the bed. Velcro straps, wires hooked to dials, clocks, and meters. It was so science-fiction sexy that, in spite of myself, I got an erection. My wife applauded.

"That gadget is wonderful!" she marveled.

"Hey, look out," I shouted. "You'll ruin the experiment."

"Fabulous," murmured my wife.

"Hey," I worried, "everything we're doing is being recorded!"

"Three cheers for science," said my wife.

Well, we broke the machine. Wires pulled off. A cable apparently short-circuited. The clock motor heaved a bussing sigh and stopped. All the meters went over the red, flickered, and came to a satiated rest.

"Fabulous," I said.

Next Monday I returned the destroyed gadget. I felt very guilty. I tried to explain what had happened to the technician. He gave me a stern look. When I asked about the aphrodisiac pill, he made an appointment for me to see the doctor.

That weekend my wife and I took some mushrooms and had a wonderful time. On Monday morning I reported for my interview with the doctor.

The old men were still in the wailing room. I raced back to see the male nurse and told him about the great sex party over the weekend. He looked at me coldly.

I told the doctor about the wonderful effects of the psychedelic. He seemed unimpressed. I asked him for the aphrodisiac pill once again. He flatly denied that such a potion existed. His position was clear. If you didn't have a circulatory problem that could be treated by normal medicine, your penile control and enhancement program was to be handled by a shrink, or your rabbi, priest, or minister.

Enlarging the Virile Member

Know, O Vizir (God be good to you!), treating of the size of the virile member is of the first importance both for men and women. For the men because from a good-sized and vigorous member there springs the affection and love of women; for the women, because it is by such members that their amorous passions are appeased, and the greatest pleasure is procured for them. This is evident from the fact that many men, solely by reason of their insignificant members, are, as far as coition is concerned, objects of aversion to women, who likewise entertain the same sentiment with regard to those whose members are soft, nerveless, and relaxed. Their whole happiness consists in the use of robust and strong members.

A man, therefore, with a small member, who wants to make it grand or fortify it for the coitus, must rub it before copulation with tepid water, until it gets red and extended by the blood flowing into it, in consequence of the heat; he must then anoint it with a mixture of honey and ginger, rubbing it in sedulously. Then let him join the woman; he will procure for her such pleasure that she objects to him getting off her again.

Another remedy consists in a compound made of a moderate quantity of pepper, lavender, galanga, and musk, reduced to powder, sifted, and mixed up with honey and preserved ginger. The member after having been first washed in warm water, is then vigorously rubbed with the mixture; it will then grow large and brawny, and afford to the woman a marvellous feeling of voluptuousness.

A third remedy is the following: wash the member in water until it becomes red, and enters into erection. Then take a piece of soft leather, upon which spread hot pitch, and envelop the member with it. It will not be long before the member raises its head, trembling with passion. The leather is to be left on until the pitch grows cold, and the member is again in a state of repose. This operation, several times repeated, will have the effect of making the member strong and thick.

A fourth remedy is based upon the use made of leeches, but only of such as live in water (sic), You put as many of them into a bottle as can be got in, and fill it up with oil Then expose the bottle to the sun, until the heat of the same has effected a complete mixture. With the fluid thus obtained the member is to be rubbed several consecutive days, and It will, by being thus treated, become of a good size and of full dimensions.

For another procedure I will here note the use of an ass's member. Procure one and boil it, together with onions and a large quantity of corn. With this dish feed fowls, which you eat afterwards. One can also macerate the ass's verge in oil, and use the fluid thus obtained for anointing one's member, and drinking of it.

Another way is to bruise leeches with oil, and rub the verge with this ointment; or, if it is preferred, the leeches may be put into a bottle, and, thus enclosed, buried in a warm dung-hill until they are dissolved into a coherent mass and form a sort of liniment, which is used for repeatedly anointing the member. The member is certain greatly to benefit by this.

One may likewise take rosin and wax, mixed with tubipore, asphodel, and cobbler's glue, with which mixture rub the member, and the result will be that its dimensions will be enlarged.

The efficacy of all these remedies is well known, and I have tested them.

—Muhammad al-Nafzawi
The Perfumed Garden of Sensual Delight
15th-century Arabic sex manual
and work of erotic literature

Thrilling Breakthrough

IT WAS AUGUST 1984 when the news we had been awaiting for hit the wires. Physiologists at Stanford University made it official. They had developed a potent aphrodisiac. The potion was extracted from the bark of the yohimbe tree of tropical West Africa. Tests on laboratory rats proved "sensational." It seemed that the surprised and delighted rodents produced fifty erections an hour. Fifty times more than normal!

The researchers announced that they were ready to begin testing the drug on humans. The news flash stirred up the predictable enthusiastic response. A spokesperson at the Stanford Medical News Bureau reported that the item had "been accorded a good deal more space and tine than most of the bureau's reports on medical progress."

The expected puritan reaction was not long in coming. One Daniel S. Greenberg, publisher of Science and Government Report, complained that "in terms of science's traditional quest for fundamental understanding, yohimbe research is pretty thin stuff." Mr. Greenberg prudishly asserted that this interest in happiness was a sign of passion, vanity, and self-indulgence—as opposed to a space shot to study the surface of Mars. The essay was widely reprinted even in the staid Los Angeles Times. The purpose of the piece was to ridicule the research and discourage its continuation.

The politics of senility prevailed once again. If any scientific commission recommended funding for aphrodisiac research, it would be opposed by the Moral Majority and the right-wing politicians. If a large pharmaceutical house tried to market a sexual enhancement drug—imagine the furor! The moralists would have another sin to denounce! Laws would be passed! The narcotic agencies would have another victimless crime to persecute.

Imagine the black market that will spring up. College campuses. Yuppie parties. Even the senior citizens' centers would be buzzing. A new drug underground? What normal, healthy person would not want to try a new love potion?

Viva Viagra®!

VIAGRA® improves erections by increasing blood flow to the penis. This causes the penis to become harder and stay harder longer.

VIAGRA® lasts for up to 4 hours. This gives you plenty of time to be spontaneous with your partner.

And VIAGRA® only works when you need it, when you are sexually aroused. After sex, your erection will go away.

—Viagra® Advertisement

9

Operation Sex Change

Do you want to be the center of attention at your next party—without disrobing or throwing up on the hostess? Here's a sure-fire tip. Turn to the person sitting next to you and ask this question: "Do you think America has undergone a change in sexual morals during the last five years?"

Almost everyone in a reasonable state of mental alertness will respond with some emotion. Most will say "Yes!" Some will say, "It depends." But everyone has an opinion. If you ask enough people, you'll get some thought-provoking answers.

My ultra-jaded friend Larry Flynt, a one-time olympic erotic athlete, groaned when I popped him the "sex-change" question. "What happened to sexual freedom and the open marriage?" he complained. "I remember this party in Atlanta around 1972. I walked into this large house and there were like a hundred(!) men and women, ya know, all nude. Drinking! Talking! Smoking funny cigarettes! Dancing! Flirting!

PETE VON SHOLLY

"And ya know what? They were all there to fuck as many new and different people as the flesh could stand! Hey, I'm speaking about middle-class folks! Lawyers. Dentists. Accountants. And their ever-loving wives! Occasionally a couple or a trio heads for the heated pool or the hot tub or the rumpus room. In every bedroom you got two, three, four couples making out on big round beds. Hey, they're swapping partners back and forth like elastic orgasms had just come on the market! Jeez, you sure don't hear of those goings-on today!"

Larry has his own theory to explain the new celibacy.

"Jealousy. Yup! Plain, old-fashioned, male jealousy stopped all the swapping."

Larry smiles to himself, a real dirty grin, and rubbed his belly and shook his head. "Okay. Imagine Max the dentist. He's happy as a toothless oyster sucking away at that cute little Georgia Peach married to the insurance agent down the street. And then he looks over and ya know what! There's his own sweetie-pie wife, her legs planted firmly in the air, merrily boffing some total stranger, a TV weather reporter from Birmingham, Alabama, with a pot-belly and a twelve-inch erection! And what's worse, she's got this ecstatic, dazed look on her face!

"Well! Dentist Max freaks out. You gotta be very secure sexually to handle that sort of scene."

Purity of Our Precious Body

MAYBE. But most people cite another obvious reason for the new morality. Fear of the new sex-related diseases. According to Susan, an attractive—one might say voluptuous—psychologist in her thirties, "It started with herpes. Then AIDS put everyone into the diagnostic mode."

"There's another health-related sex inhibitor. Female contraceptives have been given a very bad press recently. Let's face it," said Susan, "it was the pill and the IUDs that kicked off the sexual liberation of the late 1960s. But now, many women are having second thoughts about the side effects. What can a horny young woman do? Barrier devices like diaphragms are undignified, and rubbers are crude."

Susan told a story about Fred, a doctor at her clinic. "He's a real cute guy. Cool, athletic, charming. Prides him self on being a playboy stud. Now, we've been eyeing each other for a long time, and one night after work Fred invites me to his place for a drink. I'm really turned on and think-Ing some steamy thoughts as we walk into his living room. Well, one thing leads to another—erotic music, drinking margaritas, candle light, smouldering glances, secret little smiles. Fred moves next to me on the deep, soft couch, and begins caressing my neck. "Oooh! Delicious!" I relax and shift my weight to be more comfortable. Fred puts his hand on my knee. I open my legs just a little. He slides his hand up my smooth thigh slowly, slowly. I'm about to go crazy, you understand. His hand moves up more and I'm opening my legs wider. One false move and I'm his!

"At this crucial moment Fred starts thinking about his precious bodily fluids. And mine. So he pulls back his hand and clears his throat and initiates the clinical interview. He says, 'I've been tested recently for herpes, AIDS, and VI]. Including chlamydia. I'm clean as a bean, Susan. How about you?'"

Susan sighed and shook her head sadly. "Sorta puts a chill on the steamy tropical romantic climate, doesn't it!"

Frightening? Frustrating? Faddish? Friendly?

I'M SITTING IN THE POLO LOUNGE of the Beverly Hills Hotel, bored with movie talk. So I pop the sex-change question. Works like a charm. Everyone has an emotional reaction.

"It's frightening," said June, a liberal lawyer. "It's part of the Reagan conservatism. These right-wingers want to turn America into a prudish police state like Iran, with all the women in black veils and chastity belts."

"It's frustrating," said Charles, a sturdy, thoughtful aspiring screenwriter who had just moved to Hollywood. "I'm looking for a girlfriend out here, and I can't score a date. The women seem afraid of human contact. It's a lot easier to meet girls in Chicago."

"Shave your beard, sell a script, buy a Porsche. You'll have no trouble finding girls, believe me," purred June.

"This new puritanism is a fad," said Jon Bradshaw, a cynical journalist just in from the Tripoli front, "Morality fluctuates with the economy. When the stock market goes up, skirts rise. When people are worried about money, they fuck less. Period."

Bradshaw took a long sip from his scotch-rocks, unsheathed his war-correspondent leer, and scoped it in June's direction. "But I like that stuff about the Ayatollah's dancing girls with black veils and the belts. Sounds like fun."

"It's all about friendship," said Natalie, a producer's mistress. "People are definitely less promiscuous these days. Why? Because they want a relationship—not a one-night stand. And you're more likely to stay healthy and swing a movie deal if you make it with a pal."

10

Passionate Attack on Male Domination

I continued my research at Oasis, the chic new restaurant in Dallas. Richard Chase, the suave owner, sat me next to Patricia, a beautiful brunette glowing with pregnancy. The sex-change question set her off!

According to Patricia, "Women are more self-confident and assertive these days. The male department just can't deal with it. I hear it all over Texas from intelligent, beautiful, successful women. It's these gun-slinging cowboys who are causing the new puritanism. Scared by the competition. Can't get it up for a self-confident Southern woman."

Limp Defense of Male Chastity

THE GUY NEXT TO HER, a young oil executive named Nick, reacted defensively to this notion. "Men I know are more interested in making money than making a woman. Playing around is high-school and college stuff. When you get out in the real world, you realize that you drill a gal, that's one-night crude. Make a deal for a pipeline and you got almost tax-free security, assuming you survive OPEC roller-coasters."

Patricia sniffed with impatience. "What is this grease-rigger talk about drilling a woman, Nick? How about a partnership with an equal?"

"No room on my busy schedule for merger propositions. Have your lawyer ring mine, and maybe we can set up a conference call," said Nick with a nervous laugh.

Egg Wisdom

The obvious facts are that the Egg is much superior to Sperm; women far smarter than men; plants more advanced than animals.

The lowly, rooted vegetable kingdom consistently manipulates herbivores with specie-ific chemicals designed to evolve and smarten-up animals. Plants patiently and humorously select and train animals to transport, court, care for, and impregnate plants. Vegetative intelligence rides in the driver's seat of the lumbering animal body.

Even in the late 20th century males could not deal with Egg Superiority. Note how the male continues the Judeo-Christian image of the wicked-lurid-wanton-insatiably sexy female!

Men Who Make War, Not Love

THIS REALLY PROVOKED PATRICIA. "For thousands of years power has been monopolized by men who hate women. These sexists can't stand the idea that women are smarter, nicer, more loving, more beautiful than men. So they form these men's-club religions that put women down. Judaism.

Christianity. Islam. They all treat women as slaves, property, serfs, assistants to the boss. Women can't play any
active role in the ceremonies or the politics.

"Boy, y'all get out there and lasso a purty gal and brand
her and stick her in the breeding barn with a copy of the
Bible to comfort her. You know how it says: The Lord is
my shepherd! He maketh me lie down in green pastures!
The Lord strokes mah big udders. Oh praise the Lord,
cause he spraids mah laigs. He knocks me up. Glory be!

"Male monotheism! You know what that means? One
God. Whose God? My God! And guess what! He's a man!
A totalitarian, all-powerful, bad-tempered male. All the
Bibles, Korans, Talmuds agree this big numero-uno God is
of the male gender.

"And, let's face it This big-shot Allah may own the oil
fields of the Middle East, but he's a bad-ass Persian! The
last guy you'd want to have a date with. I, for one, wouldn't
go on that Mohammed's yacht, would you?

"And, to be fair about it, how about our pal Jehovah?
Who in their right mind would want him to move into the
house next door, issuing commands and ruining property
values by causing floods and turning people's wives to
salt?"

At this point Nick wiped his brow with a napkin. I did
too. Nick looked at his watch.

There was no stopping Patricia. She was on a roll. "No-
tice that in all these fundamentalist sects, the mullahs and
the rabbis and the priests actually keep the women out
of sight, behind veils, or barefoot in the kitchen, or in the
balcony of the synagogue, or in the nunnery."

At this point Nick got up and tottered off from the
table.

Patricia didn't miss a beat

"These religious men are so threatened by women that they grab swords, flags, crosses, guns, power, uniforms, anything that will make them feel adequate. They make war because they're afraid to make love."

The two other Texas ladies at the table seemed fascinated by this stuff, their eyes bulging, their pretty heads nodding in agreement. Me, I'm listening and taking notes on an Oasis linen napkin.

Sex Changes of the 1960s?

"BUT WEREN'T THINGS DIFFERENT ten years ago?" I inquired of Patricia.

"You better believe it, Doc," said Patricia. "There was that one amazing fourteen-year period between 1966 and 1980 when four thousand years of male domination were briefly overthrown. The key to this 'sixties cultural revolution' was women's liberation! The hippies represented a feminization, a sensitization of consciousness, a gentle, erotic mellowing. The hippies totally ridiculed the male power structures just by grinning at the cops.

"Here, 1986, in Rambo-Reagan America, it's hard to remember that back there in 1972, Vietnam soldiers were ashamed to wear their uniforms in public. The Texas Rangers freaked out because their swaggering authority was being ignored. The draft and the drug laws were publicly defied. Male politicians and moralists went crazy, warning about Western civilization collapsing before this wave of paganism and hedonism and wild, bra-less feminism. It was a feisty woman, Martha Mitchell, who first blew the whistle on the Nixon Watergate cover-up.

"Remember long hair? Long hair on Texas dudes! That started the country-rock scene at the Armadillo in Austin, Texas. What did that long hair mean? Men accepting feminine erotic power. Remember that cop in Houston who requested permission to grow his hair long so that he could relate to members of the opposite sex—namely, his wife?

"It was the women who made all this 'sixties stuff happen. The sexual freedom was really women's freedom. God knows the men didn't need liberation. The Judeo-Christian-Moslem double standard always let Texan men do what they wanted.

"I don't know what it was like up North, honey, but down here in Texas 'round 1969, women suddenly understood that they were free to fuck whom-so-ever they wanted and how-some-ever they wanted. It was the women who learned about slow, serpentine, Hindu, fuck-me—Buddha sexuality.

"Yup, it was the cowgirls who demanded some variation on the missionary position. And gently pulled the heads of their astonished boyfriends down to the promised land and taught white lads how to make girls feel good.

"And it was the women who demanded the new aphrodisiac drugs from their guys. Don't you remember the motto of the Hippie Girl from Galveston? Keep me high, Long Horn, and I'll ball you all night long."

Pete Von Sholly

In Celebration of the Phallis

Honen Matsuri is a Japanese fertility festival celebrated on March 15 in Komaki, a town about 45 minutes north of Nagoya, Japan. Folks haul out a large wooden penis to give three cheers to fertility and renewal. The custom is an old one that is connected to bringing about a good harvest and having babies.

The festival features Shinto priests playing musical instruments, a parade, all-you-can-drink sake, and a 2.5 meter-long wooden phallus. The wooden phallus is carried to a shrine called Tagata Jinja.

As the procession makes its way to Tagata Jinja the priests spin the phallus in its mikoshi before setting it down and saying prayers. Then the crowd is showered with small rice cakes thrown down by the officials from raised platforms.

11

What About
Sexual Liberation?

T hen **Patricia looked at me,** shook her head, and sighed. "Don't you get the point? It wasn't 'sexual liberation,' it was freedom for the two groups who were repressed by the male morality. First it was the women who took off their aprons and came out of the kitchens. Then it was the gays who came out of the closets, insisting that sex be beautiful and elegant and long and slow and graceful and funny. Mr. Redneck Macho from Fort Worth had to change his heavy-breathing, bar-room, slam-barn, steer-bull ways, and learn how to boogie and ball and fool around and be sweet and tender with his big red chap-slick.

"The Texas A&M co-ed looks at the guy and says, 'Is that a stupid jive-ass Colt 45 in your pocket, John Wayne, or have you suddenly learned how to express affection to a girl?' Hey, Buck, the penis is not a Bowie knife to be plunged into the gaping wounds of your prostrate victims! The penis is a shaft of pleasure and delightful fusion.

"What's changed from the 1960s is this: Smart, sell-confident women, after listening to Mick Jagger and Jimi Hendrix and Willie Nelson, weren't gonna go back to lying down meekly, spreading their legs anytime some Rice University frat-kid decided he wanted to get his rocks off.

"No way, Don Jose. Smart women, like that lil' ole Jerry Hall, learned to be selective and more demanding. Today, women talk about the men they know and compare them for size and fit and performance and wit and charm. And wow! Does that threaten the SMU business-administration majors! No wonder poor Nick tottered off to the, excuse the expression, men's room a few minutes ago."

The three women at the table looked at each other and smiled in some sort of secret agreement.

Aphrodisiacs for the Babes

Women seek aphrodisiacs with more relaxing properties than those in male aphrodisiacs. Many of the herbs used for women are mild tranquilizing plants that help establish a sense of peace and security that allow a woman to open up sexually.

Chocolate, of course, is a traditional love drug. Scent of roses, patchouli, pheromones and other perfumes can powerfully change brainwaves and neurotransmitters. Relaxing scents, luxurious tastes, and other sensual treats, like truffles and ginger help put many women into the mood. Don't forget massage and make sure that the oil is nice and warm with a sensuous aroma.

Scientific Poll Says
Men Different From Women

My HEAD SPINNING from Patricia's unorthodox theories, I phoned the research department and requested some hard data.

A diligent scan of the scientific literature revealed that in 1984, *Newsweek* polled students at nintey-eight campuses to find out if morals were changing. The major results: "Students are against casual sex, for fidelity in marriage, and split on the question of living together.

According to *Newsweek*, "The real legacy of the sexual revolution—and perhaps the women's movement as well—may lie in how man and women think about each other. Six out of ten say there are significant differences in the ways men and women think."

Confirming Patricia's cocky views, 24 percent of women believed that females are more intelligent than males! And only 6 percent thought men were smarter.

Pete Von Sholly

Macho Men Losing Out to Gays

PATRICIA AND OTHER SOPHISTICATED WOMEN I interviewed kept making the point that today, during this confusing time of shifting sex roles, they feel more comfortable with gays.

I asked Julia Andrews, a successful geologist from Boulder, about this, and she came up with a word that I was to hear more and more as I researched the sex-change issue.

The word is *friendship.* Many women complain that it's almost impossible to maintain a friendship with a straight guy whom you don't want to fuck. Back in the 1950s men hung out with and enjoyed the company of other men, talking about sports, hunting, careers, entertainment, business, politics. And in the old days, women busied themselves with cooking, washing, aesthetics, fashion, families, and the softer human interests. Men and women lived in different worlds.

According to Julia, "All this has changed. Many intelligent, educated, alert women these days are equally interested in careers, political issues, IRAs, adult-education courses, and prime rates. Of course, they're still into fashion and elegance and high culture; so they're looking for wide-gauge men who can share their full-spectrum interests. And a lot of men just won't get hip.

"That's where the gays come in. As a group, homosexual men make more money, are better educated, are more sophisticated than straights. They are more open to make friendships with women. They're more sensitive. And to many of us, sensitive means smarter. Like there's this professor, Bruce, in my department. He's gay. I have great times with him. We can discuss our research projects. We can gossip about office politics. He knows more than I do about French and Japanese dress designers, and he's hip on the music and movie scene. He reads cookbooks and understands how erotic eating and food can be. But the main thing is, he's sensitive to my moods, my little double meanings, my funny little jokes. There's the added advantage that, with Bruce, there's no problem about exchanging contaminated metabolic liquids."

Hasn't the Gay Scene Cooled?

MY NEXT EXPERT WITNESS was a wise old closet homosexual. Jack Black is a 55-year-old ordained Episcopalian minister. As it happens, he doesn't practice his clerical calling. Sensibly enough, he's a full professor at an Ivy League divinity school. Jack is smart, scholarly, cynical, a skillful politician. He's got a satirical sense of humor—dry; desiccated, wizened as a vulture's claw. At the moment, Jack has mixed feelings about the New Morality.

On the down side, the AIDS epidemic had him crushed. "I can't believe it," he moaned. "After thirty years of hiding in the closet, I finally see this wonderful gaypride thing emerging. Political strength, economic clout, gay churches, gay ministers preaching from pulpits! A real sense of gay power, and then..."

"Have gay morals changed?" I asked.

Pete Von Sholly

"Changed! Totally! Facts are, if you cruise the boulevard these days, the chances are 100 percent that you'll get the virus. Promiscuity is down 80 percent. The bath houses are all closed. The bar traffic is down 40 percent. And the sex practices have changed. Safe sex. People take precautions. No exchange of fluids."

On the up side, the new celibacy has done wonders for the tranquility of Jack's relationship with this gorgeous, 25-year-old, live-in lover. Now that he has become an aging man of the cloth, Jack is vigorously preaching monogamy.

"That's what happening, by God! Monogamous relationships! People are staying home with their mates. Or if you don't have a steady, then you stay home alone and watch *Dynasty* or *24*, depending upon which decade you live in."

And here in this biblical context I heard again that label for the new sexuality. Friendship.

"Friendship. Agape. Monastic withdrawal from temptation. Male bonding in the spirit of the twelve apostles. Christian fellowship. Brotherly love. Yes," said Father Jack quietly, "these days in the gay community you bugger your friend or you don't fuck at all."

12

Farewell
Sexual Freedom?

Turning from the holy to the secular side of the debate, I found that *Futurist Magazine*, true to its belief that our future lies ahead of us, has recently offered some sobering predictions about a "New Victorianism." Editor Edward Cornish expects that the uncontrollable hysteria about herpes and AIDS sweeping the world will lead to a return to romantic love. "Unable to realize their sexual longings, people will do a lot of pining and fantasizing. Popular music will move back to love themes."

- Family life will seem safer.
- Pornography will become less acceptable in polite society... but covert interest will intensify, as pornographic materials offer a substitute for risky live encounters.
- Traditional religious practices may revive.

This is probably the only time, past, present, or future, when Jerry Falwell will find himself liking the *Futurist*.

Law Enforcement View

TO RESOLVE THESE WILDLY DIFFERING OPINIONS, I went next door to get a more conservative slant on things. My right-wing neighbor, Clyde, is an assistant district attorney. He awaited me at the door, escorted me to the study, and brought me a regulation Miller Lite®. He drank standard-issue Perrier®. Clyde wears a blue suit when he sweeps and dusts for footprints around his swimming pool.

When making social conversation, Clyde stands at attention like G. Gordon Liddy giving a lecture on the Red Menace.

I wasted no time in popping the sex-change question. You don't pull punches with Clyde.

"Sex practices depend on the ethnic and class demographics of the neighborhood," said Clyde with that clipped, know-it-all, law-enforcement cadence. "In the poor neighborhoods, it's low-life, misdemeanor mischief as usual. With those people, every man fornicates illegally and immorally with everyone. Lower-class individuals still coercively obtain the sexual favors of any helpless girl they can corner. Lower-class fathers still copulate with their daughters, cousins, you name it. They're animals, pure and simple." Clyde cleared his throat. I had a strong gut-feeling that he was enjoying this conversation, in some weird way.

"Middle-class people, as we well know, tend to restrict their immoral impulses and when they indulge, at least—here he coughed—they're discreet. Thank God.

"As for the kids! Nothing new there. Spank 'em or spoil 'em, rotten through and through. As usual they're in severe need of guidance, discipline, law and order."

At this point Clyde rested his case and was excused from the witness stand.

Policeman's Son's Opinion

TO CHECK THIS OUT, I spent an hour talking to Clyde's son, Barry. He's a freshman at a small Eastern college. He said that there were nineteen kids in his dorm floor, and only two were virgins. They were both hopeless eggheads. Sexual activity tended to be located in your clique. The dopers, the jocks, the intellectuals fooled around with members of their own groups.

"You mean, friends do it with friends?" I asked.

"Yeah, for sure. Dumb kids make it with each other. Smart ones with their chums."

Basically Barry thought that all this talk about the new morality was just tired grown-ups talking wistfully about their own problems with waning sexual desire.

"Most kids think about sex all the time," said Barry with a shy smile. "At our parties, we get X-rated movies and they play all night. To give an atmosphere, you know?"

"Are you saying that teenage boys still want to fuck anyone they can get their hands on?"

Barry laughed sheepishly. "Yeah, something like that. And too often all you can get your hands on is your own best friend, you know, yourself." We both laughed.

"Haven't kids always been hung up on sex?" asked Barry. "Look at the Fort Lauderdale deal. In most Eastern schools, kids can't wait to cut loose. The weeks before spring break you can cut the tension with a knife. Girls can't wait to pile into a car and head south. Boys too. And you know they're not going to Florida to ski."

Fast Times at the High School

I WENT RIGHT TO THE SOURCE. I interviewed Marilyn, a senior in a Seattle-area high school. I was impressed by her poise and wisdom. To every question she responded, "That depends."

"Are kids doing it as much as previous generations?" I asked.

"That depends. People fool around with the kids they hang out with. Like the jocks, they make it with the cheerleaders. The girls run around with bobby-sox and pom-poms screaming, 'All the way, Bears!' And the guys are always talking about getting their rocks off and crude stuff like that. These bonehead jocks go for that sloppy stuff. Crushing empty beer cans on their foreheads before they jump into the sack, you know.

"The fraternity-sorority kids act sedate, but don't be fooled. It's a scam on their parents. These kids get dressed up in 'fifties gowns and dinner jackets and dance the fox-trot in the gymnasium, and their parents are so pleased that they're so conservative—like little grown-ups. Well, hey! By midnight at the freeway motels, those lace dresses are being pulled off and hung neatly on chairs. And the yuppie drugs like cocaine and quaaludes are being passed around."

According to Marilyn, sexual activity among high-school kids also seems to depend on the family racial and religious beliefs. Oriental kids seemed more straight, prudish, and hardworking. Kids from born-again Christian families appear to be more conservative—anti-abortion and stuff, but they all love Reagan.

"It sorta depends," said Marilyn. "It depends on how good-looking they are. If the Christian girl is a real knock-out, she tends to forget Jerry Falwell when the glands start pumping. I remember one night this kid whose folks were away gave a party, and I walked into a bedroom, and there was this real hot-looking born-again Baptist girl on her knees in front of this football player. And she wasn't praying.

"Come to think of it," said Marilyn, "the most sincere Christian kids tend to be pimpled and chubby and running low on animal magnetism to begin with."

In general, Marilyn thought that kids today were pretty selective, and laid back. "They do it, but keep it quiet. It's kinda invisible. Friendship is important."

"Is there a different standard for boys and for girls?" I asked.

"For sure. Guys that screw around a lot are considered hot stuff. And girls who come on to a lot of guys are considered wild."

13

Voices from
the 19th Century

my editor-archivist Michael Horowitz and his wife/writing-partner Cindy came to visit me in Beverly Hills. In their research for *Shaman Woman, Mainline Lady*, an anthology of the drug experiences of famous women writers, they discovered that not only had many famous female authors experimented with the drugs of their time, quite a few of them had also linked drugs with sexual experimentation. Of course, these works were often published under pseudonyms and not discovered until much later.

One of their most interesting pieces of detective work concerned Louisa May Alcott, who, while writing *Little Women* and other books, secretly published "blood and thunder tales" under various pseudonyms. Among other things, she explored the link between drug use and sexual

Louisa May Alcott

experimentation. Her most famous stories in this genre had the theme of seduction under the influence of hashish and opium.

She shared this interest with another great writer of that time, Mark Twain. Most people do not realize that the creator of Tom Sawyer and Huckleberry Finn wrote essays in praise of open sexuality. After his death his very proper wife burned most of his erotic works. At least 1601 survived—the American sexual classic of the period.

If these two icons of 19th-Century American literature could be teleported here right now, they would probably be less shocked and more fascinated than most of their contemporaries by the cool hedonism flourishing today.

> Woman is like a fruit, which will not yield its sweetness until you rub it between your hands. Look at the basil plant; if you do not rub it warm with your fingers it will not emit any scent. Do you not know that the amber, unless it be handled and warmed, keeps hidden within its pores the aroma contained in it. It is the same with woman. If you do not animate her with your toying, intermixed with Kissing, nibbling and touching, you will not obtain from her what you are wishing; you will feel no enjoyment when you share her couch, and you will waken in her heart neither inclination nor affection, nor love for you; all her qualities will remain hidden.
>
> —Muhammad al-Nafzawi
> *The Perfumed Garden of Sensual Delight*
> *15th-century Arabic sex manual*
> *and work of erotic literature*

14

New Puritanism

next, I arranged a lunch with my friend Fred. He's a black counselor in an urban high school. As far as he was concerned, there had been no drop in sexual activity.

"What new puritanism? This country is floating in a sea of sexual stimulation. How about all these R-rated films on cable beaming into homes? Thirteen-year-olds watching naked bodies writhing away! In the past you could only see this stuff at American Legion smokers. Now, it's right there in the living room! How about the X-rated CD and internet porn! Over a hundred porn movies a month coming on the market! Middle-class families screening hard-core on their home TV! And the Calvin Klein ads and the raunchy MTV clips! Madonna and Prince prancing around half bare-ass. Never before in history has an adolescent generation been exposed to such wall-to-wall sexuality. And it's all hooked up to advertising and merchandising."

Fred was worried. Not about immorality, but about the alarming jump in pregnancies. "I can't figure it out," he said. "They just won't take precautions. These kids apparently haven't figured out where babies come from! They cheer- fully get themselves pregnant, not just once, but several times. These are not just unwanted pregnancies. They're unconscious pregnancies.

"I can't understand it. They have all this information about sex. Manuals and how-to books and magazine articles, and yet they're not using the data to manage their lives."

Fred thought that television and films may have dulled consciousness and desensitized kids from the real, flesh-and-blood world. "You know, they watch Rambo in the theatres, bare-chested, sweating, gunning down armies of gooks, and they watch Obama smiling and waving while he's sending flying robots over Pakistan and Afghanistan, and they don't realize the difference. They seem to think that sex is having aerobic fun rubbing body parts together like on the TV screen. They don't seem to connect sex with the deep significance of the procreative act. It's the 'ol pre-AIDs attitude. Sex is healthy exercise, good for your self-esteem—like dancing and jogging and bowling.

> Conjugal love involves the appeal of body and instinct, the power of feeling and affectivity, the aspirations of spirit and will. All of these aim at a union beyond the flesh, a union of heart and soul. This definitive mutual self-giving demands indissolubility, faithfulness, and openness to children. In this way, natural conjugal love expresses Christian values.
>
> *Catechism of the Catholic Church*

"As I remember, it was different in the 1960s. It may sound naïve to say this today, but during the hippie years there was a big sense of the sacredness of life.

"Consciousness was the key. Everything was very important, Holy! They even called psychedelic drugs sacraments. Can you believe that!

Pete Von Sholly

"And sex was an act of yogic cele-
bration. A resurrection of the body!
Sounds corny to say this, but there
was an undeniable reverence for life
in the 1960s. Antiwar. Peace and love,
baby! People talking about raising
consciousness. Kids putting flowers
in the barrels of National Guard rifles.
Ecological concern for the oneness of life. Which led to
vegetarianism. And goofy, pompous idealism. And gee-whiz
spiritualism. But it's a statistical fact that the teenage
suicide rates were way down in the 1960s and so were the
unconscious pregnancies.

"In the 1960s there was almost no personal violence.
People were blissed out, I guess. All the violence was gov-
ernmental. Take Woodstock, for example. Can you imagine
it? For three days five thousand kids in gangs rolled around
in the mud, listening to rock music, and apparently not one act
of violence. Rape was unthinkable. Fighting was uncool, man.
"By contrast, during one week of spring break back in the
1980s, seven college kids died in Fort Lauderdale, falling
off hotel balconies, drunk. And in the Palm Springs Easter
riots, kids roamed the streets, drunk, pulling bikinis off
women in cars.

"Imagine the low state of consciousness of these kids
when they get drunk and fuck. No wonder there are so
many unconscious pregnancies.

"I'm talking about the coarseness, the meanness, the
thoughtlessness, the materialism, the low consciousness of
recent years. Kids seem to be fucking more and enjoying it
less, if you ask me."

So said Fred.

Women Not to Be Enjoyed

A leper

A lunatic

A woman turned out of caste

A woman who reveals secrets

A woman who publicly expresses desire
for sexual intercourse

A woman who is extremely white

A woman who is extremely black

A bad-smelling woman

A woman who is a near relation

A woman who is a female friend

A woman who leads the life of an
ascetic

And, lastly the wife of a relation, of
a friend, of a learned Brahman,
and of the king.

—Mallanaga Vatsyayana
Kamasutra

Pete Von Sholly

15

Is There
a Generation Gap?

W **ell,** based on more than a hundred interviews and an extensive review of the available scientific data, I conclude that the amount of sexual activity today, as always, depends on age. The older you are, the less you think about and indulge in sex. The wild gang of rock 'n' rollers who were our models in the past have unquestionably cooled down. I'm only talking about the living here, so to speak.

But look at those kids! If anything they're doing it more and earlier. A *Newsweek* poll revealed that, by the age of 23, only 10 percent of college kids were virgins. And adults, as always, are wringing their hands about youthful promiscuity.

There does, however, seem to be one consistent sex change in our American culture.

The quality and variety has improved. Especially for Americans in their twenties and thirties. They're more sophisticated, and more selective about sex. Frenzied promiscuity is certainly out of fashion, especially among gays. The highly publicized orgies, the swinging, the swappings of the past turn out to be mainly media hype. It ain't happening at all now.

Everyone is talking about it less. The current attitude around the 7-Eleven reading Jerry Falwell's biography. You'll locate New Women in that third of the population that is better educated, upwardly mobile, and more sophisticated.

The rise in teenage pregnancy is also for real, but mainly in urban ghettos and among the underclass.

Yes, Virginia, There is No New Puritanism

WHAT ABOUT THE NEW CONSERVATISM that you've been reading about? It's a media hype. Network executives and magazine editors creating fads to boost newsstand circulation, reacting to the wishful thinking of vocal moral minorities.

Reformers and moralists come and go, but sexual attitudes today still reflect the basic, earthy American virtues of tolerance, good humor, common sense, and fair play. Sure, the right-wing fanatics continue to wring their hands at the idea that people are still pursuing life, liberty, and happiness. But rest assured; American women are not going to let themselves be put in veils and chastity belts. Americans still want to have fun and enjoy life.

There is no new sexual conservatism.

Nor is hedonism destroying our republic. Your daughters are safe, Archie Bunker. They are more realistic. They are smarter. They want to fuck friends, not strangers. And that has to be beneficial for the mind, for the body, for the soul, and for the American way of life.

16

Digital Activation of the Erotic Brain

A **young woman** named Vicki is alone in her bedroom. She sits on the edge of the chair with her legs spread wide. She is looking intently at a computer terminal on the desk in front of her.

Vicki is a novice cyberpunk. She is using an electronic-communication device for her own private pleasure, without institutional or government authorization.

At the moment, Vicki's eyes are fixated on letters that wiggle across her screen. Vicki blushes with excitement. She is breathing heavily. She squirms into a more comfortable position, not taking her optics off the letters squirting across the screen like spermatozoa.

Suddenly the words stop.

Vicki smiles. With her right hand she begins typing letters on the keyboard in front of her.

Vicki In Arousal Mode

Vicki's words now appear on screen:

```
┌──────────────────── RECEIVE ────────────────────┐
│                                                  │
│   OH RON . . . I FEEL SO BAUDY WHEN WE'RE ON LINE.│
│      YOU'RE SUCH A GOOD TRANSMITTER!             │
│   AND YOU DOWNLOAD SOOOOO GOOD!                  │
│      OOOH YOU'RE SO COMPATIBLE—LET'S INTERSCREEN . . .│
│   I LIKE YOUR BIG, STRONG HARDWARE. (WHERE?)     │
│      I WANT TO PUT LOVE-BYTES ON YOUR KEYBOARD   │
│   AND SLIDE YOUR JOYSTICK INTO MY F-SLOT.        │
│      TELL ME HOW YOU WANT ME TO ACCESS YOU.      │
│   PRESS ENTER AND I'LL BOOT UP MY MALE-MERGE FUNCTION!│
│   OOOH! DISK OVERLOAD! MY SYSTEMS ARE CRASHING!  │
│                                                  │
└──────────────────────────────────────────────────┘
```

Cybernetworks

VICKI IS USING HER COMPUTER to boot up and artfully program the lust circuits in her brain. Her software is linked up, via telephone, to the Amiga of a man named Ron whom she has never met. Well, never seen in the flesh.

Vicki and Ron first interscreened in a computer network. They started off quite sedately, both contributing ideas to a public-access conference on "CIA Terrorism in Nicaragua." They came to like each other's ideas; so they agreed to chat on a private line—just the two to them exchanging electronic signals to each other through their computers.

Well, one thing led to another—as it often happens in male female conversations. At first they joked and flirted. Then they started having imaginary dates. First, they'd select a movie. Afterward they'd select a restaurant, then type in their wine and dinner orders. While waiting, they'd discuss their reactions to the movie.

Then as the imaginary, transcontinental night-on-the town started winding down.

Vicki wasted no time typing her answer.

Well, the next steps were quite predictable. Both got slowly carried away. Vicki put a compact disc in the boom box. Ron lit the fire. Slowly, timidly, they started typing out their sexual fantasies, step by step descriptions of foreplay, sly suggestions about what they would like to do to each other, and what each would like have done. Like most computer kids they are smart, inventive, and very shy, but just then, they were getting bolder and saucier.

Whew! After fifteen minutes of this cyber-aphrodisia, they had constructed the most romantic, elegant, sophisticated, all out, wanton, mutual sex affair imaginable. Prefrontal nudity, floppy disco, sloppy disco, hard disco, cyberporn.

Imagination, the creation of mental images in the brain, was realized in electronic form. The computer screen became the vehicle of their inner steamy, fantastic, cyberotic party.

17

Zen of Cyberfuck

Ron and **Vicki** were using the power of modern electronics to brain fuck, i.e., to link up their nervous systems by means of carefully selected signals transmitted between their computers by the phone lines. These lovers have thus become members of a fast growing, erotic network—those who have discovered the intimate possibilities of cybersex. The secret is this: Computer screens have a powerful, hypnotic ability to create altered states in the brain. Two people communicating through their fast feedback computers can access a range of brain circuits arguably wider than can be reached by bodily contact.

Everything exists as a nervous system.

This is because the brain and the computer work the same way—in the language of electric impulses, of light.

The Body-Brain Relationship

ALL OF US, I am sure, want to improve the wondrous pleasures that come through the soft tissues and silky membranes. Tender hands. Soft, probing fingers. Wet lips. Soft, curving thighs. Sweet, satin mounds and bulging protuberances.

Human beings are robots operationally programmed by 1) neurogenetic templates, 2) neural imprints, 3) social conditioning.

No one is implying that the basic skin tissue hardware is in any way outmoded. Nothing can replace the kissing, cuddling, licking, nuzzling, nibbling, smelling, murmuring, sucking, joking, smoking, honey moaning, fondling, biting, entering, and receiving the tender exchange of love's soft bruises.

But, however enjoyable, our bodily contacts exist for us only as registered in our brains. We sense the touch and taste and perfume and the membrane softness of our lovers only in clusters of electric signals picked up by our neurons and programmed by our mindware.

All events in nature, including human behavior exist for us only as registered, recorded and mediated by the Brain.

The nervous system is the instrument for receiving, integrating and transmitting knowledge, the Brain is the center source and sole transceiving instrument of consciousness, learning, memory, behavior, intelligence and pleasure.

The dimensions, variables, divisions, groupings, lawful relations defined by the sciences and all other fields of human endeavor are based on, filtered through, determined by the receptive, integrating and transmitting characteristics of the Brain.

—*Timothy Leary*
The Game of Life

Quantum Sex

PEOPLE WHO USE COMPUTER SIGNALS to arouse each others' sexual desires have stumbled onto the next evolutionary step in human interaction: quantum sex... cyberlust... multimate ... infocum. Electronic arts. Radio shacking? Broderbund? The Commodore, after all, is the commander of a fleet of pleasure craft!

People who communicate via computer phone link ups can reach amazing levels of

> In cybersex, speed—not size—matters. You don't want to leave them with the impression that you're an inattentive lover. With all due respect to the Pointer Sisters, the Internet is no place for a lover with a slow hand.
>
> —Billy Shakespeare
> *The Complete Idiot's Guide*
> *To Having Cybersex*
> *With Other Complete Idiots*

intimacy. This was a surprising development. Most respected newspaper columnists, pop psychologists, liberal ministers, and conservative moralists had been warning that computers will depersonalize humanity, alienate us more from each other.

Media experts made the classic, dreary conservative mistake: trying to explain the future in terms of the past. Bureau stats and managerials, their eyes firmly fixed on rear view screens, think of the computer as a machine. A metal product of the industrial age. Sexless. Hard. No one, except certain decadent, black leather, transvestite, hair dyed, mechanico freaks in the decaying slums of factory suburbs, fans of kinky, techno punk musicians from Lou Reed, Talking Heads, and Devo, to Pornos for Pyros, Babes in Toyland, Pearl Jam, Ministry, and White Zombie, would think of using machines with ball bearings and transmissions and smoky, metal parts to enhance sexual and romantic experiences.

Ultimate Organ of Pleasure

BUT THE COMPUTER IS NOT A MACHINE. It's a silicon subcircuit of an electronic brain. It's an interpersonal communication device, a cyberphone.

Now, think about it for a moment. The brain has no eyes, ears, lull lips, strong thighs. The brain is a powerful knowledge processor packed away in, and protected by, the bony case of the skull. The same is true of the computer, a powerful thought processor packed away in, and protected by, the metal case.

Both the brain and the computer receive, sort, and output "ideas" in clusters of electric on/off signals.

The brain, lest we forget, is the ultimate pleasure organ. And the personal computer, if we know how to use it, is a powerful organ for neurosexual intercourse.

When two people link up via computers, their "naked" brains are interscreening. Directly. All the complicated apparati of bodily contact—garter belts, bedrooms, zippers, bras, contraceptives, body parts—are bypassed. Your electronic tongue can slide along the Q links into his soft pink receivers with no clumsy props to get in the way.

Your Brain is in Control

Brain chemicals control your sexual response, so any drugs or conditions that alter your brain chemistry can alter your sexual response. Dopamine is a neurotransmitter important for pleasure and reward. An increase in dopamine activity may enhance the sexual response. Conversely, blocking dopamine may compromise the response.

Serotonin is a neurotransmitter responsble for
feelings and emotion. Low serotonin levels can lead
to depression and   other conditions.
Widely pre-   scribed medica-
tions, like   fluoxetine (Pro-
zac®), parox-   etine (Paxil®),
and sertra-   line (Zoloft®),
keep levels   of serotonin
circulating   longer by
preventing   its uptake
and break-   down. While
these drugs   increase serotonin activ-   ity and relieve
depression,   sexual response
may be diminished.

Complexities of Tissueware

SUPPOSE THAT RON AND VICKI had met at a discussion group
and started dating. First at the coffee shop. Then maybe
a cocktail lounge. Then dinners and movies. The first
fumbling steps at intimacy—holding hands, knees rubbing
under the table.

What to wear? The familiar mating-ground questions.
My place or yours?

Then the complicated dance of mutual seduction. The
nagging worries of the person with no more than average
sexual competence.

He wonders: Shall I make my move now?

She wonders: Will he think I'm a slut if I grab a
handful?

He wonders: Is she smart? Is she pretty enough?
Can I get it up? Does she like to transmit
head? Receive head? 300, 1200 or 2400
baud? 32-bit clean?

She wonders: Is he hip enough? Too hip? Handsome enough? Can he get it up? Can he boot
me up the way I want it? Who is this guy
anyway?

He wonders: Who is this babe anyway?

Worry. Worry.

Telesex Encourages Brain Play

DIGITAL FOREPLAY is a wonderfully natural way for two
people to start their mating dance.

Why use the word "natural" to describe communication
via phone linked computers? Actually, almost every animal species has developed distance courting, tele arousal
signals to pave the way for the eventual sweaty, writhing
contact of genital sex and the ejaculation of sperm.

Insects telecommunicate their sexual desires with
amazing gusto. Every little cricket you hear scraping his
violin string wings on a hot summer night is telling the
neighborhood ladies exactly how he'd like to do it to them.
The horny boy cicada is talking directly to the brain of the
neighborhood girls.

The chemical scents—pheromones—of the female dog in
heat are like telephone messages telling every lusty male with-
in miles how the horny young bitch smells, looks, and tastes.

The Birds and Bees Do It

BIRD SONGS ARE A COMPELLING WAY for arousing sexual desire.
At the right time of year, usually in the spring, the male song-
bird's body swells with testosterone—the male sex hormone.
He bursts into song. He sends a long distance, mating dating

message that is picked up by every female in the neighborhood. The song boots up the sex circuits in the female's brain
and she suddenly starts thinking how nice it would be to have
a lusty guy around to nibble her willing neck and stroke her
soft, feathered body with his wings and climb on top with his
wiry, strong, warm body and open her up with his straining
hard modem and make her feel just the way her brain tells
her a young bird should feel in the springtime.

How well a male song bird learns his song affects
the female's mating response has been confirmed
by research. Female birds use song-learning ability
as an indicator of male quality. When female birds
prefer well-learned songs as demonstrated by show
a shivering of the wings, the lifting of the tail and a
characteristic call.

Neurotumescence

FERNANDO NOTTEBOLIM and his colleagues at Rockefeller
University discovered that "shakes the conventional wisdom of brain science ... Nerve cells in birds go through
giant cycles of birth and death... At the time of hormonal
changes, the brain anatomies change. The specific portion
of the forebrain responsible for singing, which is large in
the spring, becomes half as large in the fall... Furthermore,
talented canary singers have larger specialized regions
than those deemed less talented.

In other words, the brain is a sexual organ that can swell
and subside like the pink membranes of penis and vagina.
And the steamy brain gets turned on by compatible signals.
And the songbirds who can give "good phone" grow bigger
brains! What an advertisement for quantum sex!

Four Phases of Sexual Response

* Sexual desire (libido) is dependent on hormonal factors and mental stimuli involving all your senses: touch, sight, taste, smell, and sound.

* Sexual excitement or arousal is characterized by penile erection and vaginal lubrication. These are the result of an increase in blood flow to the area and an alteration in your brain chemicals.

* Orgasm is the climax of sexual pleasure and is in response to hormones and brain chemicals.

* Resolution involves the release of sexual tension; you know it better as "afterglow."

Telephone Sex

TELECOMMUNICATED SEXUAL MESSAGES have become a standard courting technique in industrial-urban societies where boys and girls don't get to meet and look each other over around the village square.

How do city kids get to know each other, test each other out as mating partners? The use of the telephone and texting by courting adolescents is an inevitable step in human evolution. Q-sex a just adding a new dimension to the conversation of good, honest boy-girl lust. Appletalk is a direct way of turning on the teenage circuits of our brains.

Cybernetics of the Adolescent Brain

NEW CIRCUITS OF OUR BRAINS activate at the onset of puberty when the body undergoes changes almost as dramatic as the metamorphosis of caterpillar into butterfly.

All sorts of new bumps and protuberances emerge on the nubile body. Breast begin to swell and strain to be caressed. The little worm-penis of the school boy grows into a swelling, red tube of incorrigible desire. New circuits of the brain suddenly turn on, flooding the body with impetuous hormones and hot mating juices. The teenager becomes obsessed with sex.

Psychologists tell us that the teenager thinks of sex several times an hour. Involuntary erections strain the jeans of the embarrassed lad. Hot steamy currents of desire lash the body of the perturbed young lady—she screams at rock stars and swoons over the pinups of handsome movie stars.

Let's face it, teenagers are often coarse, crude, and insensitive to the delicate needs of others. In the desperate grip of passion, they trip over themselves and hurt each others' feelings. That's where electronic foreplay comes in.

Electronic Foreplay

TEENAGERS USE ANY MEANS possible to turn on and channel their sexual drives. Boys study magazines like Hustler, letting the pictures and the text trigger off their imaginations. Girls devour magazines about rock stars and movies actors. The pictures activate the swelling "sex areas" of the brain. Remember the horny songbirds?

Moralists condemn solitary sex and try to suppress erotic-aesthetic publications that people use to trigger off their imaginations and boot up the "sex areas" in their brains. The Moral Majority gets convenience stores to ban *Penthouse, Playboy,* and *Hustler.*

18

Cyber Spin the Bottle

There's no stopping the sperm-urge. Teens will always explore sexuality. The more forbidden, the more fervent their seeking. Like cyber Dick and Jane Tracys, teens use hand-sized phones with cameras to say, "I'll show you mine, if you show me yours!"

As an evolution of texting, "sexting" is risque but seemingly safe. Miss Lolitas can flirt outrageously without fear of being grabbed and dragged off to the woods. And why not when hormones are surging and the Egg is calling out, "I want you"?

Sure, it is okay for boys to experiment with their new-found equipment. Afterall, boys will be boys. The Moral Majority denies that little girls are sexual beings. Teenaged girls experimenting with sexual self-representation brings out the inner puritan.

Who hasn't posed and postured in scanty clothes—even buck naked—in front of a mirror? With endless no cost photos in fabulous full color, digital cameras transform shy

Guy: "I got blueballs, Ba B."
Girl: "Yeah? Wut do u want?"
Guy: "Is NE1 else there?"
Girl: "No. Wut do u want?"
Guy: "2 c u."
Girl: "K. Cum over?"

kids into sex kittens and hunky studs ready to star in the next porn flick. Inevitably, teen pin-ups are uploaded by sperned suitors and widely promulgated to cyber lounge lizards. But at 16, who cares?

> *Sexting:* Text messaging someone in the hopes of having a sexual encounter; begins with casual, transitioning into highly suggestive and even sexually explicit flirting. Like phone sex except through texting. Explicit pictures may be included. Term used by adults who are out of the loop, and not by the individuals actually sending the messages.

The Puritan Police see something sinister. Around the country teens are being prosecuted for pornography and dubbed "sex offenders". Back in my day this would have been equivalent to incarcerating kids for playing Doctor, Spin-the-Bottle, or Strip Poker.

Ear Sex in the Confessional Box

BACK WHEN I WAS A TEENAGER in the dark ages of the 1930s, we were warned in the sex manuals that masturbation caused nervousness, mental breakdown, and eventual brain damage. The Catholic Church was pursuing its insane policy of stamping out genital pleasure and preventing the "sex areas" of my brain from swelling. I remember the kinky conversations in the confessional box.

I would kneel in the dark booth and whisper through the screen into the invisible ear.

"Forgive me, Father, I am guilty of impure thoughts."

"Which impure thoughts, my son?"

"I thought about making love to my cousin Margaret because of her dimpled knees, to Dr. O'Brien's wife because she is blonde and has big boobs, to Clara Bow, to all the members of the chorus line of the Radio City Rockettes, to a girl I saw on the bus. . ."

"That's enough, son," Father Cavenaugh sighed. "Have you used any sinful books or magazines?"

"Yes, Father." *Spicy Detective. Spicy Adventure. Spicy Western. Film Fun. Captain Billy's Whiz Bang Joke Book. Atlantic City Bathing Beauties. Hollywood Starlets.*

"Enough, enough!" cried the flustered priest. "Such books and magazines are occasions of sin. You must destroy them."

"Yes, Father."

"Now, say a heartfelt Act of Contrition. And as your penance, say five Our Fathers and five Hail Marys."

This whispered "tell and listen" ritual did little to prevent the "sex areas" of my brain from growing. Might as well try to stop the testosterone drenched song birds from singing!

Confessions were heard by bored or sex-tortured priests because it was their only erotic contact. They obviously got off on it. In a way we sinners were giving the good Fathers aural sex by kneeling there in the dark box, whispering our sweet little dirty secrets into the warm, open, trembling ear of the priest.

Teenagers today spend hours sexting dirty jokes and flirting because it's a safe and calm way to explore erotic interests without being swirled into grappling scenes. They stimulate each others' imaginations, exploring, and experimenting with erotic signals. Cybervamps: Telephone Call Girls

The telephone-sex call services advertised in the back of magazines like *Hustler* are another step forward into the art and science of brain sex.

Sandi's phone-sex ad invites you to "Talk dirty to me! I'll rub my nipples hard. I want to cum with your phone fantasies."

Anal Annabelle promises, "I'll spread myself wide open and give you all of me, Big Boy."

"Beg for it!" Says Mistress Kate. "I know what you desire."

"Climax with me! I'm hot, wet, and waiting!" murmurs Lisa.

Immoral Exchange of Electrons?

MAYBE YOU'VE FELT THIS STUFF IS A BIT KINKY. Perhaps you felt that telephone call-girl sex is a masturbation aid for lonely people with low self-esteem.

Maybe not. The moralists and spoilsports want us to feel guilty about phone sex. Bureaucratic cyborgs are automatically offended by any frivolous, hedonic, dilettante use of technology for personal delight. Phone are leased to us by Ma Bell or Verizon® to help us become better citizens and to call home at holidays.

Actually, neurophone sex link, if employed with a light touch-tone, can be a wonderful way to learn how to become skilled at telefucking.

Tapping the Erotic Memory Banks

THE ARCHIVES OF OUR BRAINS carry electronic memories of our earliest teenage passions. So why not receive them, turn them on, and enjoy them at will?

The trick is this: You learn how to format your brain to receive the cues, the sensory signals that activate your horniest 16-year-old memories. You can use a telephone call service or do it with a friend. Ask her or him to whisper to you the coded names and phrases of your first crushes. The songs of your heated season of rut. You'll find yourself booting up your adolescent circuits with the teenage access codes. You are performing a neurolinquistic experiment. You're executing a self-hypnotic age regression. You are "commanding" your own brain to expand the "sex areas."

Now here is some good news: Your brain is apparently eager to oblige. Your brain wants to be stimulated, opened up, caressed, jacked into by a sure hand.

Your brain hates boredom. If you keep your brain repeating the same old reality tape, month after month, your brain will sigh and give up on you, just like a neglected lover.

For many people, cybersex—using the telephone or computer or ipod to arouse the brain—is easier than running around like a horny robot, pulling clothes off and on, jumping in and out of sacks with strangers. Unless you are incredibly cool and poised, it's difficult on a first date to teach a new computer how to turn on your imagination and the start acting it out, while at the same time trying to master the private signals that turn his or her brain on.

Computer Simulations

CYBERSEX IS A RELAXED WAY OF LEARNING how to explore this brand-new frontier of cybercourse. The computer is a wonderful appliance for simulations and "as if" experiments. The hottest selling software in the hobbyist market

is simulation games. Flight simulation: practice takeoffs and land-
ings. Submarine commanders: act
out the Battle of the North Atlantic. Wall Street simulations: pre-
tend you're a hot-shot broker.

If you don't use your head for your own pleasure, entertainment, education, and growth, who will?

Now, if it's all right to use
software to simulate war, why is it
not okay to simulate the most im-
portant game of all? Why not get on line and link up with
the brain of your partner? Murmur teenage sweet nothings
into her brain—ROM? Stick your floppy disk into his cere-
bral software and whisper exactly the things he wants to
hear?

Simulation: You are back again in your parent's house
flirting with your high-school crush! And while you are taking advantage of your parent's absence by disporting naked
in the rumpus room of your cerebellum, give yourself some
credit. You are a neurosexual pioneer! You belong to the
first generation of your species to use your magnificent
brain as a sexual organ. Without guilt. With healthy curios-
ity. And a desire to please your cybermate.

You are learning to use your
head, to take over the pro-
gramming of your bored
brain. Surfing your own
brain waves.

PETE VON SHOLLY

Cybering

Cybersex and brain-fucking could be key to freedom and growth. If you don't use your head for your own pleasure, entertainment, education, and growth, who will?

Cybersex enables you to be totally anonymous while indulging in the safest sex possible.

Men and women at home and in the workplace everywhere enjoy cybersex is a pastime. These passionate exchanges vary from suave romantic messages to blunt graphic dialogue. Both couples and singles engage in cybersex.

In a chat room a cyberseducer may send another chatter a text message: "Wanna cyber?" During cybersex or "cybering" lovers at different computers in difficult locations role play sexual fun and games while texting their erotic actions and hot responses. Sometimes lovers meet up in fantasy towns, like Second Life, as avatars.

How do you do it?

WHEN INCREDIBLY EXCITED, typing with one hand is pretty frustrating. Using an inexpensive microphone lets the sexpot you're getting it on with can hear your excitement and know that he or she's turning you on. Masturbating while describing your experience to your partner evokes vivid, visceral images in your lover's mind.

Boot up your sexy brain, your primary erogenous zone— the most powerful aphrodisiac. Dial up your cyberotic mind. Text passionately titilate your cyberlover's heart.

Webcams

WITH A WEBCAM lovers can really go all the way. You can watch as your lover diddles and cums. Why go to a fern bar looking for love when you can meet up at commercial webcam websites where cybervoyeurs watch each other masturbate on camera. Exhibitionistic couples can perform on camera for the enjoyment of others.

Particularly hot cybering is a simulation of "real" sex, were cyberlovers make the experience as close to real life as possible, with partners taking turns texting descriptive, sexually explicit passages. Allows couples to carry out sexual experiments they would not try in reality.

Unleash Your Imagination

IMAGINATION IS THE KEY to hot cybersex. Be creative with your language whether you're texting or using a mic. Tailor your language to your lover's preferences. Some cyberbabes, for example, like nasty, vulgar language, while others like a sensuous walk on the beach.

Cyber seduction takes refinement and technique as does a face-to-face experience where looks count for a lot. In cyberomance looks are part of the fantasy. So engage your main sex organ—your brain. Be specific, give details and also vary your pillow talk. For example, if you are seducing a dude by telling him you will do him on his exercise beach while his pals watch, name a real gym. When coming on to your babe with a glass of red wine, use the name of a particularly expensive brand. Women especially are turned on by this sort of detail because you appear experienced and cultured.

> "For women, the best aphrodisiacs are words. The G-spot is in the ears. He who looks for it below there is wasting his time."
>
> - Isabel Allende

Cybersex is easy and convenient. You don't have to go to a fleabag motel. Easy to have a quick romp when coming home from work. Cyberlovers may be established couples who make love in real life who, when separated meet in cyberspace for a "quickie". More often the people who met in cyberspace do so solely to cyberfuck. Hardcore cybering enthusiasts stay in character throughout the affair, which may evolve into phone sex, and "real meets" in character. These "avatars", as they are sometimes called, develop lengthy pasts for their characters to make the fantasy more life-like.

Cybersex offers a greater degree of anonymity than does phone sex, while allowing horny cyberlovers to meet partners. Cybersex workers do engage in cybersex in exchange for both virtual and real-life currency in online worlds, like Second Life

Intimate Strangers

Whirling through endless electronic realms
You launched your lust upon electric currents
Of cresting cybercircuits, wanting a fantasy,
A lover who would create a magic moment,
A mystery-space in time, oblivious as to why,
Escape into a virtual world of intimacy.

You sat behind a computer, obscured,
An anonymous stranger seeking bliss
In a virtual kiss, cock-throbbing caresses
For the strong, hard thrusts into an imaginary
Woman writing as wildly as the fire
Engulfing you in the flames of desire,
Searing the screen where you stared
At passionate words racing hotly through
An artificial tunnel where distance disappears,
And there's only you and her, man and woman,
Locked in a primal dance of deathless energy.

Later, drained and dazed, you tell her
(Though you too suspect it's not true)
That virtual intimacy is quite normal,
And it's safe for total strangers
To share a dream of sexual thirst
Which spans the continents onscreen.

Somehow discomfort sets in, she seems
To bridge the cold void of emotionless
Oceans, the many wires and phone lines
Separating you both, asking questions
You'd rather not answer, nor ask
Of her either. Yet she persists & requests
You reveal more than you meant to --

It's like waking the next bleak morning
When a one-night stand stays too long.
Disentangling yourself from the intimate

Strangeness, which you could have prevented,
You exit, flushed and slightly ashamed:
It was only a brief, mindless event,
You and yourself, touching and stroking;
She was a bright screen lit by lust
And you were as needy as she was...
You tell yourself it was not real,
Only a blind jerkoff in a virtual world,
A fragmentary collision of intimate strangers.

—Cara Swann
Cyber-Charade©1997

Cara Swann: authoress1@juno.com

Is It Cheating?

OH YEAH BABY! Sure cybersex is a source of sexual freedom
and fulfillment. But beware. It can led to the break-up of
marriages and partnerships. Cybersex can be very powerful and overwhelmingly real to the participants.

We're all loose and liberal free love lovers until your girlfriend is masturbating in tandem to the thoughts, images, and words of another dude and he is describing how he's going to get you babe off. And she loves it! Then you suddenly get quite prudish and possessive.

For years, news media have been reporting about the worrisome phenomenon of "virtual affairs" - people who have prolonged intimacy over the Internet. Sometimes the other side is a kind of "pen pal" whose true identity is known. With increasing frequency, it is a fantasy character who achieves intimacy with another fantasy character. The participants generally view these parallel relationships as harmless, but real-life spouses (male and female) do not always agree and these affairs have been implicated in a large number of divorces.

—Asher Meir
Jerusalem Post

20

Teledildonics

Cyberotic enthusiasts use electronic sex toys controlled by a computer, called teledildonics or cyberdildonics, for remote mutual masturbation. Physical touch sensations are transmitted between lovers over a data link. Sometimes prerecorded movies are synchronized with the toys' actions by a software script.

Teledildonics was coined by Ted Nelson in the 1980s, and popularized in 1991 by Howard Rheingold in his book *Virtual Reality* where he described having virtual reality sex over the internet.

By 1997 there were already some 10,000 adult sites online generating $1 billion a year. A few hot sites brought in more than a million bucks a month. Today there are hundreds of thousands of websites and we are involved in a multi-billion dollar industry.

In the 1990's media artist Stahl Stenslie built a full body cyber suit, but the FDA forced it off the market as dangerous to health because they said it could interfere with pacemakers.

Homemade Sex Toy

FLASHIEBACKIE:

"There has always been decadence," the propri-
etor of a novelty items store is saying. "The Industrial Revolution was just a missing link between the
Roman Empire and this portable electric artificial
vagina."

Captain Mediafreak is filming this sales pitch to a
customer, played by Tongue Fu.

"I wouldn't use it myself—I'm a happily married
man but we still live in a democracy. These products
were originally intended to collect semen from bulls
for the artificial insemination of cows, but they're
perfectly safe for humans. However, their use is
not recommended if you are a victim of premature
ejaculation."

"How would I use this artificial vagina?" Tongue
Fu asks.

"You plug it in your AC wall socket. Simple
enough. This model has a temperature control
mechanism which approximates natural vaginal
warmth. You can increase the temperature all the
way up to Unbearable. You must lubricate the instrument for maximum efficiency and pleasure.
We recommend our own special lubricant which is
formulated for optimum viscosity. You may choose
to partially pressurize the instrument before penetration. It has a wide range of adjustability, from a
diameter of two inches to entirely closed. This dial
here regulates the tiny waves of stimulation which
set up a pulsation pattern that aids in ultimately trig-
gering the ejaculatory nerves. Incidentally, we also
have a model which plugs right into the cigarette

lighter of your favorite automobile. Sometimes you feel like a spot of organismic pleasure while waiting on line for gasoline. Or even in traffic. On the way home from work seems to be a very popular time."

"How does the deluxe model differ?" Tongue Fu asks.

"The deluxe artificial vagina has rubber folds which, upon inflation, roughly simulate the labia majora and the labia minora just as these tissues are when swollen in actual sexual passion. It also features a three-speed bulbocavernosus muscle which contracts rhythmically. Moreover, it is covered by a soft fabric with skin-like texture—flesh colored—you have your choice of Caucasian, Negroid or Asian. You would probably prefer the Asian. Incidentally, sir, our deluxe model has a special sphincter attachment. Do you happen to suffer from flaccid penis? Of course, this is an optional feature. . . ."

—Paul Krassner
Tales of Tongue Fu

The Thrill Hammer has giant tentacles coming out of it, with a computer mounted on a gynecological chair like a threatening monster that might penetrating every orifice in our body. Allen Stein who invented the Thrill Hammer has probably produced more orgasms than the sexiest porn stars, without even touching anyone.

Possibilities in sex machines are only limited by your imagination and your budget. You can get anything from bondage accessories to full force feedback haptic control with virtual environments. Yeah, sex machines are pricey but can you really put a price on pleasure?

Timothy Archibald, author of *Sex Machines: Photographs and Interviews*, described sex machines as "cylindrical, almost painful-looking metal contraptions that had a big flywheel and a thrusting shaft and like a wooden base. They were very rough, and nothing was very polished about them. And then there was this phallic dildo at the end."

Another machine called the Pile Driver was invented by Scott Ehalt. It consists of two vertical shafts of steel with an enormous dildo mounted on it and an engine attached. He told his nosey neighbor that it was a machine for poking holes in sheetrock.

A popular sex toy is the RealDoll, created by Matt McCullen in the late 1990s. It is an amazingly lifelike sex partner, complete with optional robotic hip gyration and MP3-enhanced sounds of pleasure.

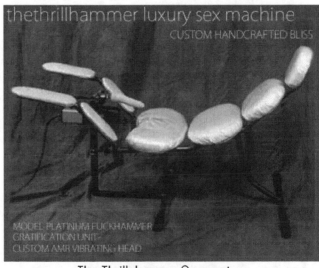

The Thrill-hammer Orgasmatron

Seattle entrepreneur Allen Stein invented the Thrill-hammer Orgasmatron, an antique gynecological chair with a futuristic built-in vibrator that is controlled over the Internet by the woman's partner in cybersex.

The Virtual Sex Machine is a device that fits over the penis that generates a variety of sensations in synch with sexual activity portrayed on the computer screen. The device, developed by Eric White, uses an ingenious combination of vacuum pump, a back-and-forth motor, and a stimulator at the penis tip that White says "adds a little extra zing." For an even more intense experience the solo cyber lover can purchase virtual reality goggles to provide a more realistic environment than a computer screen.

Hummmmm..... I'll leave you with Vale's pentrating questions:

> Since the Internet has lowered the financial bar giving practically "zero sum" access to texts and graphics depicting the most imaginative sexual fantasies and practices since the world began, what does this do to the human imagination? Where is your own unique identity in all this hurricane of mediated electronic images?

> Until the individual dream can be captured and saved to computer memory storage, the human imagination, with or without drugs and computers, will remain the ultimate, miraculous, cinerama-conjuring wonder machine capable of inspiring our most favorite memories and pleasurable recollections.

> And for each person alive on planet earth, memory is the supreme judge of a life lived. Who did you love? What were your favorite experiences to cherish and recollect in tranquility? What did you create that you are lastingly proud of?

Timothy Leary was a world-renowned psychologist, a West Point student, a defrocked Harvard professor, a relentless champion of brain-change, a stand-up philosopher, a Federal "criminal" and a counterculture guru famous for saying, "Turn on. Tune in. Drop out!".

Leary's charisma and radically humorous nature often captured the attention of the world. While waving one of Leary's books a judge at sentencing hearing called him, "the most dangerous man on the planet". Leary continues to be an inspiration for millions of freedom-loving and free-thinking people throughout the world.

U nderground pundit V. Vale of RE/Search Publications has been giving his counterculture viewpoints for over 30 years in his lectures, panel discussions, publications, and radio and television appearances. He has traveled the world to share his alternative views on everything from contemporary art to swing music. Counting J.G. Ballard and W.S. Burroughs as his main influences, he is now influencing the next generation of popular culture and academia alike. The tattooing and body piercing/body modification world acknowledges Vale for "making it all happen" through his book, *Modern Primitives*. The lounge music resurgence also has Vale to thank for the trend of vintage music reissues with his "Incredibly Strange Music" books and CDs; a new trend in sideshow/midway performance art has been catalyzed by his publication of *Freaks: We Who Are Not As Others* and *Memoirs of a Sword Swallower* as well as *Modern Primitives*. Jello Biafra called Vale's initial publication, *Search & Destroy* "the best Punk Rock publication, ever." The list goes on, so please catch up with Vale at *http://www.researchpubs.com*.

BOOKS published by V. Vale: Industrial Culture Handbook; W.S. Burroughs, Brion Gysin, Throbbing Gristle; Incredibly Strange Music Vol. 1 & 2; Incredibly Strange Films; Pranks!; Pranks 2; Modern Primitives; Angry Women; RE/Search Guide to Bodily Fluids; Torture Garden; The Confessions of Wanda Von Sacher-Masoch; Wild Wives; High Priest of California; Freaks; Memoirs of a Sword Swallower; Me and Big Joe; Here To Go; Leary On Drugs; Burning Man Live; Swing: the New Retro Renaissance; Search & Destroy Issues 1–11; J.G. Ballard; J.G. Ballard: Quotes; J.G. Ballard Conversations; Modern Pagans

RE/SEARCH PUBLICATIONS
20 ROMOLO PLACE, SUITE B
SAN FRANCISCO, CA 94133
(415) 362-1465
info@researchpubs.com
http://www.researchpubs.com

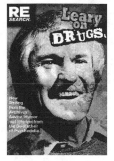

Ronin Books for Independent